The MAP

An Actor's Guide to On-Camera Acting

Stef Tovar

T0346487

APPLAUSE

THEATRE & CINEMA BOOKS

Guilford, Connecticut

Applause Theatre & Cinema Books
An imprint of Globe Pequot, the trade division of
The Rowman & Littlefield Publishing Group, Inc.
4501 Forbes Blvd., Ste. 200
Lanham, MD 20706
ApplauseBooks.com

Distributed by NATIONAL BOOK NETWORK

British Library Cataloguing in Publication Information available

Library of Congress Cataloging-in-Publication Data

Names: Tovar, Stef, author.
Title: The map : an actor's guide to on-screen acting / Stef Tovar.
Description: Guilford, Connecticut : Applause Theater & Cinema Books,
2021.
| Includes index. | Summary: "Actor Stef Tovar, seen on-screen in
Contagion, Widows, Employee of the Month, Chicago Med, and more,
teaches you the 'foreign language' of on-camera acting. Tovar gives actors
a practical, step-by-step technique on how to audition for and book on-
camera acting jobs-and what to do once on set" —Provided by
publisher.
Identifiers: LCCN 2021023875 (print) | LCCN 2021023876 (ebook) |
ISBN 9781493060931 (paperback) | ISBN 9781493060948 (epub)
Subjects: LCSH: Motion picture acting. | Television acting.
Classification: LCC PN1995.9.A26 T68 2021 (print) | LCC
PN1995.9.A26 (ebook) | DDC 791.4302/8—dc23
LC record available at https://lccn.loc.gov/2021023875
LC ebook record available at https://lccn.loc.gov/2021023876

"Luck is what happens when preparation meets opportunity."

—Seneca

Contents

~

Preface

When I left my undergraduate university acting program and moved to Chicago, I had a solid knowledge of the craft of acting. I received good training and was lucky to begin my on-stage career right away. However, I never studied on-camera technique. Even today, acting programs are packed with movement training, voice and speech, and scene study, but most don't give students a blueprint for approaching on-camera work. Auditioning and booking an on-camera job, and what to do when you book that job, are things you just have to figure out for yourself.

I started auditioning for on-camera jobs in Chicago in the 1990s, and I didn't have much success. I let it go and focused on theater. I wanted to book on-camera jobs, but I didn't know how to approach them. When I moved to Los Angeles in 2000, I had an agent and started auditioning for commercials. It still took two years of auditioning and getting called back before I booked a job. I didn't have the right technique. Through trial and (mostly) error, I learned. I eventually filmed lots of commercials, a couple of feature films, and one episode of *Judging Amy* (as a cop with three lines) before moving back to Chicago after the birth of my son.

Back in Chicago, I began to book more television and film jobs and felt a growing confidence (granted this was over twenty years after I finished college). I started coaching actors auditioning for on-camera jobs because I wished someone had told me how to do it when I was in my twenties. I wish I knew then what I learned through my years of mostly mistakes (and some successes). I was driven to share my experience with others. I got great satisfaction from creating a technique that worked and helped other actors book jobs.

I used to focus on the acting only—what your character wants from your scene partner (objective), tactics, and so on—thinking that if I was a good actor, I would win the role. It wasn't until I began to treat on-camera acting as another language that things really began to click—both as an actor and acting coach.

What I learned over the years from my experience as an actor in front of the camera and from talking to casting directors, directors, agents, and doing hundreds of on-camera coaching sessions is this: on-camera acting isn't just about being a good actor. It's really like learning another language, the language of on-camera, and applying it to your acting skill set. And that on-camera language really has *nothing* to do with what you studied in college or in the various Meisner or audition classes you've taken. I created the MAP to be a simple, practical technique that will help you own an audition room and give your on-camera audition the authenticity you need to start booking instead of just getting put on hold.

In addition to my on-camera MAP technique, this book will serve as your *Roadmap* to how you receive, prepare for, and audition for on-camera jobs in television, film, and commercials and what you do on set after you book a job. You'll also learn how to self-tape auditions. You will take the journey from taping yourself at home on your cell phone to being on set for a commercial, television show, or film. This book was written in the middle of a global pandemic. Self-tapes have since become the *only* way casting directors see actors for roles for not just television and film but also theater, so learning how to make a great self-tape is imperative. My technique can also help you with your virtual callback sessions.

I will also cover what they don't tell you about booking a job and showing up on set from the perspective of a day player. Day players in television, film, and commercials are actors that are hired "for the day," mainly co-star roles, who are important to the story but do not carry the film or television show. Why that perspective? Because in many ways, the co-star's job is the hardest—and it's also most likely to be the first job you'll book. I'll share some of my stories of being on set in "Confessions of a Day Player" style to help you gain perspective of what the job of an on-camera actor entails when executing a day player role.

I'll also spend some time on Acting 101, so that those of you who haven't studied will have a background for it. You will need to be able to analyze a scene and understand the job of an actor in order to succeed on-camera. But make no mistake: you can be the greatest actor around, and if you don't learn the language of on-camera acting, your audition simply won't translate in the "box." I call it the *box* because that's what it is: a box in which you have a minute or two (sometimes much less) to show them what you've got from your elbows to the top of your head and win the role. Sounds glamorous, doesn't it? Yet every actor dreams of starring on screen alongside the Matt Damons and Gwyneth Paltrows of the world. How does one get that job? Well, I'll share that story with you, but first we are going to dive in and learn this new language called on-camera acting and how to speak it.

Enjoy the ride—you've got this.

—Stef Tovar

CHAPTER ONE

~

How to Get
an On-Camera Audition
Casting Directors, Agents,
and How to Get Started

I'm on set for the film *Contagion* getting my microphone put on me when I see Gwyneth Paltrow arrive. She is five foot nine in her bare feet, is wearing sunglasses, and has a Starbucks cup. She totally looks like a movie star even though she's supposed to be playing a sick person. I'm *still* waiting for someone to tell me there has been a mistake and Robert Downey Jr. will be arriving shortly to play the role of ER Doctor—not me.

Then Matt Damon walks on set. He looks just like a regular guy. He's looking over his pages, casually says hi. Little do I know that we are going to hit it off, and at the wrap party, he and I will bond and hang out the whole night. Right now, I'm pretty much in awe and intimidated by him.

Then they bring me to set: a fully functioning ER where we will be shooting. In the room is just a bed with Gwyneth in it, some hospital equipment, a woman playing a nurse, an on-set doctor to give advice, Matt Damon, and Oscar-winning director Steven Soderbergh, who is both directing and working a single camera on his own. "Ok, let's rehearse." he says.

I guess I'm really doing this.

I had never met Steven prior to walking on set. I certainly never rehearsed or even read the script out loud with Matt or Gwyneth. I actually didn't even audition for the role of the ER doctor (eventually they gave my doctor a name: Dr. Arrington). When I left my college acting program, this moment seemed impossible to even imagine. So, how did I get here?

You'll get a detailed account of how I landed my role in *Contagion* at the end of this book, but what is the first stop on the road to getting on set? Let this book be your roadmap, and I'll be your guide. In order for you to book a job in television or film, you have to actually get an audition for a television show, feature film, or a commercial. How does one make that happen? That is the first stop on our roadmap from getting an on-camera audition to being on set.

No matter where you choose to live and begin your career, you need to understand that casting directors are the gatekeepers of television and film jobs. They are hired by producers to cast their television show, feature film, or commercial. You have to put yourself in front of a casting director to be seen for on-camera jobs. Generally, casting directors only take submissions from talent agents. A talent agent's job is to send their clients out on auditions for casting directors. They submit their actors to various casting directors for jobs in television, film, commercials, and theater.

This book is for those of you who are studying on-camera for the first time. You are most likely an actor in an undergraduate college program or a professional who is just starting out, so you may not yet have an agent. How does one get an agent?

Getting an Agent

Once you decide which city to settle down in, you'll want to do some research on the different agencies there. The bigger the city, the more agencies you'll have to choose from. In Los Angeles and New York, your goal will be to have two agents—a theatrical agent (one that sends you out for jobs on television shows, films, and theater) and a commercial agent (who sends you out only for commercials and perhaps voice-over work). In smaller markets like Chicago and Atlanta, you'll have one agent who will send you out for both. In the two larger markets, there are triple the number of casting directors, and thus the need for two specialized agents.

The best way to get an agent is to have someone who already has an agent vouch for you (and also vouch for the agency) and "walk you in." By that I don't actually mean they physically walk you in the door of the agency. They will send an email or call their agent and say, "You should really give this person a look—I can vouch for them" and send along your picture and résumé. I'm going to assume that if you are reading this book, you understand that an actor's "business card" is a picture and résumé: a professional head-shot and résumé detailing your experience. I've put an example in the back of the book for you as a reference.

If getting walked into an agency is not possible for you, you need to send your picture and résumé along with a cover letter to various agencies in hopes that one calls you in for an audition. It's a tedious process that takes time. Some undergraduate acting programs do "showcases" where they will sometimes invite agents and casting directors to come and watch your work. I've known lots of actors who have gotten agents from showcases. If you are out of college and happen to be in a show, invite agents and casting directors to come and see you.

Should you sign with the first agency that wants to sign you? Do your research—make sure the agencies you send your materials to are reputable. Do they represent union talent and are they SAG-AFTRA franchised? Talk with actors who are represented by them. If it's a bigger agency, will you get lost there? If it's a more boutique agency, will they have the ability to get you into all the casting director's doors? How many of your "type" do they represent? You may interview with just one agent, but you'll usually have to be approved by all the agents in the office. After you've done your research, choose the agency that you feel best about. Wherever you sign, always remember this: agents are commission based. You don't pay them until you book a job. Their commission comes out of your earnings from the job they book for you. You should never pay an agent out-of-pocket, and they should not require you to take a specific class or use a specific photographer in order to sign with them.

Can I get an on-camera audition without an agent?

Yes, but only if a casting director calls you in directly: either from a showcase, a play or musical you are performing in, or a mailing you sent out. Casting directors are always looking for new talent, and they will be proactive on finding good actors—but the best way to get through a casting director's door is having an agent push you through.

Do I have to be in the union (SAG-AFTRA) to audition for a film, commercial, or television show?

No, you do not. Most likely if you are just starting out, you will not be in a union of any kind. But that doesn't mean you can't audition for and book union on-camera jobs. You can. There is also a lot of non-union work these days too. I am a proud member of both SAG-AFTRA (Screen Actors Guild – American Federation of Television and Radio Artists) and the Actors' Equity Association. When I first started out, I worked non-union jobs, but now that I'm a member of the union, I can only work on jobs sanctioned by one of the two unions. To understand the rules of unions, what is required to join, and so on, check out sagaftra.org or actorsequity.org.

A Word about "Type"

As an actor in a university program or someone who is just starting out in the business, you've probably been told what your "type" is by someone, either a teacher, director, fellow actor, a friend, or a family member. Having an awareness of your type is important as you pursue an agent, as they will look at you as a specific type and send you out on auditions according to what they believe your type is. Are you the romantic lead? The quirky best friend? I'm a true character actor now, but when I was just starting out, I didn't have a grasp on what my type was—and when I moved to Los Angeles, it affected my learning curve and success.

I moved to Los Angeles to pursue television and film work in 2000 and thought I'd be like Ross on *Friends* or some kind of lead on a television show. My mother warned me. I told her I was going to move to L.A. after a successful ten years in Chicago doing theater. She said, "So you want to move to L.A., huh?" "Absolutely," I said. She said, "Well, you're cute in Chicago, but you're going to be ugly in L.A."

She was not incorrect (though she was just trying to protect me as she always did). It took me a couple of years to grow into and become a "Young Dad" type. And during that time, I went on a lot of auditions and callbacks. I got really frustrated. I was always getting called back but never booking. Luckily, my agent stuck with me. She said, "If you're getting called back, you're doing everything right. Keep at it." I finally got a little older and grew into my type, and when I did, I began to book a lot of commercials. Spots for Nexium, AT&T, Scott's (lawn care products), Long John Silver's, Jack in the Box, Travelocity, and others. By 2005–2006, I would be up against the same five to eight guys you would see booking every commercial. Most of the time they booked the jobs I was up for, but I was also starting to take jobs from them. Eventually they started getting more television co-star work and I got more of their commercial work.

I think the success I found on-camera in Los Angeles happened when I began to identify and understand my type and what roles I was truly being considered for. When I was in Chicago just doing theater, my type meant a lot less. And as actors, we don't want directors or casting directors seeing us as only one thing. But it was different auditioning for television and film in Los Angeles. You'll hear this a lot in this book: casting directors for television and film don't want actors—they want real people. You need to walk in and just be the role—not "act" it. That's part of what knowing your type means. In Los Angeles in the early 2000s, I read very midwestern, blue-collar, "young dad" type. There were a lot of pretty people in L.A., and I wasn't one of them; but I learned and understood what my type was, and I carried that into an audition room with me proudly. Your type won't be the only thing you can play. In fact, many of you will want to push to play *against* your type, but if you understand and embrace what others may consider your type to be, you will have the ability to use it to your advantage in the audition room and when you are trying to find an agent.

Auditioning for Agents

If an agent is interested in you, they will call you in to audition for them. You should treat auditioning for an agency the same way you would an on-camera audition for a casting director. Agents will want to see if you have some theater credits on your résumé, but they will look at you and ask themselves, "Can I send this actor out on auditions for television and film jobs?" They ask that because although theater can be lucrative (especially if you work on Broadway, a national tour, or at a LORT [League of Resident Theatres] theater), they will make more money from you if you can book on-camera work.

In the fall of 2019, I played Yossi Bellin in the Chicago premiere of the Tony Award–winning play *Oslo* for TimeLine Theatre at the Broadway Playhouse. I worked for twelve weeks and made a nice weekly salary. Then in January of 2020 I booked an episode of NBC's *Chicago Med*. I had a decent role (a top-of-show guest star) but just a few scenes, and I only worked a total of four days on the show (even though I was contracted for ten days). I made more in four days on that television show than I did working twelve weeks on a play. That is why agents want to make sure you can book on-camera work.

If agents want to see if you can do television and film work, it is important to make sure one of the pieces you do when you audition for an agency will work as an on-camera audition piece and apply the technique in this book to it. This means doing a song (if you do musical theater) and a Shakespearean monologue will not show an agent that you can audition for *Law and Order*. Make sure one of the pieces you do for your agency audition is more suited for television and film.

When I say find a piece that is suited for television or film, I mean a piece that is served by a delivery that is less theatrical and more real. What do I mean by theatrical? One where you would typically use large gestures, raise your voice, and emote. You can do a Tennessee Williams monologue for an agency, provided you apply the rules of on-camera acting detailed in this book to your audition. Your goal is to show the agency that you could be cast on a television show, in a film, or a commercial. So, doing a highly theatrical piece or a Shakespearean monologue will probably not serve that goal. You also don't want to choose material that everyone has seen (like a scene from a famous movie like *The Godfather* or a Marvel movie). It takes some work, but there are lots of books out there that compile monologues for you. Spend some time researching and finding a great monologue that fits you well—something that fits your type and that you would be cast in by a casting director. And make sure it is a piece that will look good in the "box" (see chapter 4).

I'll reference various television shows, films, and specific actors throughout this book as examples of good on-camera technique. One I use often is the television show *Breaking Bad*. The show is fantastic in terms of storytelling and the way it is shot, but the performances are incredible. Watch Bryan Cranston's performance in the "I did it for me" scene of *Breaking Bad* (you can do an internet search for it). There is an economy of movement, voice, and delivery (that I will discuss how to do in chapter 5) that makes it a perfect example of great on-camera acting. That's what you want to show a potential agency. Find a piece that accomplishes that goal.

Treat the audition and interview for an agency as a job interview, which goes both ways. You are interviewing them as much as they are interviewing you. It's a two-way relationship. Take the pressure off yourself to "perform." Just be yourself.

Remember: ultimately your agents work for you. Make sure that whatever agency you wind up signing with, you have a good relationship with them. You're able to reach out and ask them questions or advice on your career. Actors frequently ask me what questions they should ask when they have an interview for an agency. I always say, ask them how they like to communicate. Do they prefer a phone call or email? You want to make sure you have access to your agents and aren't afraid of asking them questions that could help you.

Getting the Audition

You've chosen a city to start your career and you've obtained an agent (or have a good relationship with a casting director that calls you in for auditions). After signing with an agent or being called in directly by a casting director, you finally get an audition! Congrats!

You've arrived at your second stop on our roadmap. Here's what you can expect:

For the purposes of this book, I am focusing on auditions for "day player" roles: roles in television or film that are hired "for the day." These are also known as "co-star" roles. These roles are important to the story but do not carry the film or television show. You are being hired to be in service of the stars of the show and the story they are telling. This will most likely be one of the first jobs you audition for and book, so that is why I chose to start here. These roles are also more difficult to execute than you may think.

You will most likely get a phone call and an email from your agent or the casting director. They will first call you and schedule a time for you to see the casting director. They'll call and say, "Hey, Stef. We have an audition for you tomorrow at Karge/Ross Casting for *Empire* (the Fox television show). 12:20 p.m. Can you make it?" Or you may be asked to submit a "self-tape" for the role (more on that in chapter 7). You'll tell your agent or the casting director if you can make the audition or not. Then you'll receive an email with the detailed information you'll need, including the date and time of your audition, address of the casting director's office, and the "breakdown." If you are asked to turn in a self-tape, they will give you explicit instructions of what they want you to do for your self-tape.

Reading the Breakdown

The *breakdown* is a show business term for both on-camera and theater that breaks down the details of the project for you, including who is producing it, who is directing it, what network it will be on, the storyline, the character descriptions, and what they require of you if they are asking you to self-tape for the role. Breakdown

Services is an online resource that casting directors use to post auditions for projects.

Your agent will send you an email with a condensed version of the full breakdown. It will contain an attachment that will include your "sides" or the scene you'll be auditioning with, and it looks something like this:

Appointment for: Stef Tovar—EMPIRE #620
APPOINTMENT INFORMATION FOR: EMPIRE #620
Client: Stef Tovar
Status: Called Out (meaning the agent has reached out to you by phone)
Date: Thu, Mar 12, 2020
Time: 12:20 PM CDT
Role: Lawyer
Male. 50s. Caucasian. One of the finest legal minds in New York. He/she analyzes Diana Dubois' evidence. Co-star.
Rate: Sag scale plus 10 percent
Material: Emailed
Read For: Casting
Notes: this is the last Empire episode
Parking: street parking
PROJECT INFORMATION
Project: EMPIRE #620
Episode: 620
Type: Television
Director: Sanaa Hamri
Writer: Brett Mahoney and Stacy A. Littlejohn
Studio: FOX / Twentieth Century Fox Television
Executive Producer: Brett Mahoney, Brian Grazer, Danny Strong, Francie Calfo, Lee Daniels and Sanna Hamri

So what do you do with this information?

Many actors will just skip right to the sides and start memorizing their lines. We'll discuss how to approach the sides next, but first, take a good look at the breakdown and ask these questions:

- *Is the show currently on television?* If so, watch a few episodes if you can. With *Empire*, this was easy. It was a hit show! Easy to take in a few episodes to understand the tone of the show and who the main players were.
- *Who is the director? What other work have they done?* So her name is Sanaa Hamri. After looking her up, I see that she came up making music videos. Maybe I should prepare for the fact that she may not be comfortable directing actors with text? Maybe she'll have a great overall vision for the shots and episode, but not be interested in detailed scene work with actors.
- *What does my character description say? Are there any details in there that will inform what I wear to my audition?* Should I wear glasses or no glasses? Makeup? These descriptions can be all over the map and many times *not* helpful at all. They also can be insulting (looking for a dumpy, unattractive boring guy). You will sometimes be shocked by the character descriptions—it's as if they don't think actors will see these.
- *What is the plot of the show, and how does my character fit into it?* You will know this by watching episodes—especially the pilot that sets up the series. But if the show has been on television a while, watch recent episodes and get as much info as you can.

Don't skip this part! Walking into an audition room or sending in a self-tape fully informed by the breakdown is vital. You want every advantage when you audition—being fully prepared is the best way not only to win the role but to combat nerves.

Now that you've got some good background information on what on-camera project you are auditioning for and your sides, how do you go about giving a great on-camera audition?

~

CHAPTER TWO

The "MAP" Technique

Creating a Map
of Your On-Camera Audition

What Makes a Great On-Camera Audition?

For our third stop on our roadmap, I interviewed casting directors, agents, and directors and asked them one question when I first started coaching actors: "What makes a great on-camera audition?" Everyone said different versions of the same word: *authenticity*. What makes your audition stand out and be authentically *you*? Here's a hint: It's definitely not the lines you memorize.

When you get the call from your agent, check your email, read the breakdown, and look at the sides for an audition that you sometimes have less than twenty-four hours to prepare for, you focus on one thing: memorization—memorizing your lines and getting "off book." But what wins you the role is not your ability to memorize and say the lines in order. Every actor auditioning for the role you are auditioning for is going to do the same thing: memorize the lines and repeat them back in the order they are on the page. What is it that wins you the role if it's not how you say your lines?

It's what are you doing *in between* the lines that sets your audition apart from others.

Great on-camera acting is all about watching you *think*. What are you thinking when you are listening and not speaking? It all lies in the beats. Those beats are where the magic happens, and I'm going to show you how to create a map of them. This might be the most important stop on your roadmap to being on set.

You create beats or moments in between the lines where we get to see your character think and make decisions—where we see the inner life of your character. By creating a map of these beats and focusing on them more than your memorized dialogue, you give your audition authenticity. It is in these beats that you win the role and book the job.

The MAP is the audition technique with which I have found the most success for myself and hundreds of my students. I made it easy to create because actors have enough to think about when it comes to executing an audition. I call it a MAP of beats because you use a symbol like an asterisk * or a plus sign + to point out where in the script you need to take your time and nail certain moments. When you look at a copy of your sides after filling in your beats, it should look like an actual map. Focus on those moments when you audition rather than just the lines you're memorizing—because those moments or beats are more important and will ultimately make you stand out. This is not to say don't memorize your lines—do the best you can to get off book. However, it's the beats where you really make your audition authentic and win the role.

The MAP can be used for theater as well. As with any audition, we start with the text. Once we have a handle on the text using the MAP, we will discuss how to apply the language of on-camera to our audition and make sure it looks good in the "box."

But first: the text.

How to Create a MAP of Beats for Your Audition

When you receive your audition copy or "sides," analyze the scene asking three questions:

- Who am I talking to?
- What is my relationship to them?
- What do I want from them?

You also want to look at what the "event" of the scene is and write it down. This is especially helpful if you are a co-star on a television show or film. An event of the scene might be something like this: "Joe gives Detective Halstead a key piece of evidence to help him crack the case." Or "Elliot tells his daughter that he would do anything to save her mom." I'll go into more detail in chapter 3 on how to analyze a scene. After you do your brief scene analysis, identify where the beats are in the scene.

A beat should be *active*. It is not a moment of inaction or silence. It's a moment where we see a shift in your character, where we see your character make a decision or have a discovery. It is not a *pause*. It's an active moment where we get to watch you think. Be as specific as possible when fleshing out these beats in your scene.

Another way to think about the beats: it's as if you are thinking your subtext or inner monologue instead of speaking it. In Shakespeare, characters frequently speak their inner monologue—or private thoughts—directly to the audience. That's called a soliloquy. But on-camera, many times you have little or no dialogue and still have to convey major parts of the story with just your eyes. You do this by thinking—thinking specific thoughts and allowing the camera to catch them through the use of beats.

Let's look at this short, two-page scene for example—FRONT DESK AGENT. This role will most likely be a single day of shooting for a television show. This technique works for larger roles too.

FRONT DESK AGENT

SCENE 1

INT. SOHO HOUSE WEST HOLLYWOOD - WAITING AREA - NIGHT

Gigi is sitting on the couch in the waiting area downstairs.
She watches as two MANAGER TYPES wait to be let in. The FRONT
DESK AGENT is early 20s and just rude enough for it to be not
infuriating.

start
                    FRONT DESK AGENT
            If you'll take the elevators behind
            you, you'll find her up the main
            stairs when you get inside.

The managers walk to the elevator. Two TRENDY GIRLS in tight
dresses totter in and are waved through by the Front Desk
Agent. Gigi looks at the RECEPTIONIST, then checks her phone.
Texts: **Babe, ETA???? My phone's about to die.** She puts her
phone back on airplane to preserve the remaining fuel.
Without her phone she has no armor. This feels awkward.

INT. SOHO HOUSE WEST HOLLYWOOD - RECEPTION - 40 MINUTES LATER

Gigi is at the desk with the Front Desk Agent, typing on a
computer. Gigi tries to assist --

                    FRONT DESK AGENT
            I'm sorry, but I can't tell you if
            a member is already here--

                    GIGI
            Dumont, with a T. You tried that?

                    FRONT DESK AGENT
            I tried it all the ways.

                    GIGI
                (thinks, then)
            Small chance he put me under a
            different name.

                    FRONT DESK AGENT
            Did he.

                    GIGI
            He sometimes puts my birth name on
            lists, as a bit. It's not funny and
            has never been funny. It's Jean
            Dubrowski.

                    FRONT DESK AGENT
            I'm going to need you to spell
            that.

$\frac{1}{2}$

Figure 2.1.   Audition sample sides for a co-star role—page 1.

FRONT DESK AGENT

                   GIGI
        Jean. J-E-A-N. Dubrowski. D-U-B-R-O-
        W-S-K-I. Dubrowski--

             FRONT DESK AGENT
        I'm sorry, the last part again?

Gigi is trying not to be mortified when she sees a guy
behind her looking at her.

end

2/2

Figure 2.2.   Audition sample sides for a co-star role—page 2.

Exercise

Your audition should have at least three beats:

1. Your moment before or what I call your *need to speak*. As your audition begins, why are you speaking? What has happened that has made you speak? That is your need to speak and we must see it at the top of every audition. This beat happens moments before the tape starts rolling and someone says, "Action!"

2. Find a beat somewhere within the scene, even if you only have two lines. The second beat is harder to identify than the need to speak, but every scene has one. It may be your reaction to your scene partner's line. Every scene is different, so it could be before, during, or immediately after your next line, but find one. Find one at the top of your scene to slow you down as well. Allow yourself to *take your time* and use the second beat to help you accomplish that.

3. The *button*—EVERY scene for every audition (television, feature film, commercials, and even theater) needs a button. Otherwise, your scene ends with you staring blankly after you finish your last line. The button accomplishes two things: it lets casting know the audition is over and gives a "lift" to the scene by giving your character one final thought. You see buttons on television shows and in commercials all the time. Your audition should always have one.

(See FRONT DESK AGENT scene scored with beats below.)

In order to make sure the beats you are taking are active and specific, practice the scene by saying out loud the thoughts in your

FRONT DESK AGENT

SCENE 1

(*) 1st BEAT
NEED to SPEAK

INT. SOHO HOUSE WEST HOLLYWOOD - WAITING AREA - NIGHT

Gigi is sitting on the couch in the waiting area downstairs.
She watches as two MANAGER TYPES wait to be let in. The FRONT
DESK AGENT is early 20s and just rude enough for it to be not
infuriating.

start

                    FRONT DESK AGENT
          If you'll take the elevators behind
          you, you'll find her up the main
          stairs when you get inside.

The managers walk to the elevator. Two TRENDY GIRLS in tight
dresses totter in and are waved through by the Front Desk
Agent. Gigi looks at the RECEPTIONIST, then checks her phone.
Texts: **Babe, ETA???? My phone's about to die.** She puts her
phone back on airplane to preserve the remaining fuel.
Without her phone she has no armor. This feels awkward.

INT. SOHO HOUSE WEST HOLLYWOOD - RECEPTION - 40 MINUTES LATER

Gigi is at the desk with the Front Desk Agent, typing on a
computer. Gigi tries to assist --

(#) 2ND BEAT

                    FRONT DESK AGENT
          I'm sorry, but I can't tell you if
          a member is already here--

                    GIGI
          Dumont, with a T. You tried that?

(#) 3RD BEAT

                    FRONT DESK AGENT
          I tried it all the ways.

                    GIGI
                 (thinks, then)
          Small chance he put me under a
          different name.

(#) 4th BEAT

                    FRONT DESK AGENT
          Did he.

                    GIGI
          He sometimes puts my birth name on
          lists, as a bit. It's not funny and
          has never been funny. It's Jean
          Dubrowski.

(Start Typing)
                    FRONT DESK AGENT
          I'm going to need you to spell
          that.

1/2

Figure 2.3.   Audition sample sides for a co-star role—with beats—page 1.

FRONT DESK AGENT

                        GIGI
            Jean. J-E-A-N. Dubrowski. D-U-B-R-O-
            W-S-K-I. Dubrowski--

**@ 5th BEAT
(stop Typing)**
                        FRONT DESK AGENT
                I'm sorry, the last part again?

        Gigi is trying not to be mortified when she sees a guy
        behind her looking at her.

    # Button   **end**

$\frac{2}{2}$

Figure 2.4.   Audition sample sides for a co-star role—with beats—page 2.

beats. They should sound like extra dialogue that you will eventually think and not speak. Do the following exercise:

1. Write out the dialogue you will be thinking in your beats.
2. Then read the scene saying the thoughts you've written out loud along with your lines given to you on the page.
3. Then do the scene as written—simply thinking the thoughts you were previously speaking.

See the FRONT DESK AGENT scene with your character's thoughts written in below. This exercise is critical to understanding the difference between an active beat (which we want) and a pause (which we do *not* want).

The masters are great at allowing an audience to see their thoughts: look no further than Daniel Day-Lewis in *The Phantom Thread*. The New Year's Eve scene—where he rushes to find Alma at the party and in two minutes without speaking a word of dialogue, he wins the scene, obtains his objective, and you understand their relationship perfectly.

Once you have chosen your beats, as best you can, flesh them out. Most of us won't have two years to prepare for a role before we are in front of the camera like Daniel Day-Lewis. You'll sometimes have two hours. But the more you understand the choices, discoveries, and thoughts you are having in your beats, the more confidently you will be able to execute them in the audition room. Don't just try to memorize your lines: memorize your beats—they are more important than the words you are saying. Think about the moments you're going to nail in the audition room rather than the lines you need to recite.

Is there a wrong place to insert a beat? You'll know the answer to that question when you write out your beats as unspoken dialogue. When you write out your beats as actual thoughts, the level of specificity in the beats prevents you from making choices that

FRONT DESK AGENT

SCENE 1

(*) 1st BEAT
NEED to SPEAK

INT. SOHO HOUSE WEST HOLLYWOOD - WAITING AREA - NIGHT

Gigi is sitting on the couch in the waiting area downstairs. She watches as two MANAGER TYPES wait to be let in. The FRONT DESK AGENT is early 20s and just rude enough for it to be not infuriating.

THOUGHTS FOR BEATS

start

FRONT DESK AGENT
If you'll take the elevators behind you, you'll find her up the main stairs when you get inside.

MANAGER-TYPE ASKS ME: "I'M SORRY. WHERE DID YOU SAY VERONICA WAS?"

The managers walk to the elevator. Two TRENDY GIRLS in tight dresses totter in and are waved through by the Front Desk Agent. Gigi looks at the RECEPTIONIST, then checks her phone. Texts: **Babe, ETA???? My phone's about to die.** She puts her phone back on airplane to preserve the remaining fuel. Without her phone she has no armor. This feels awkward.

SEEING GIGI WALK UP TO MY DESK

INT. SOHO HOUSE WEST HOLLYWOOD - RECEPTION - 40 MINUTES LATER

Gigi is at the desk with the Front Desk Agent, typing on a computer. Gigi tries to assist --

(*) 2ND BEAT

"UGH. THIS ANNOYING WOMAN AGAIN."

FRONT DESK AGENT
I'm sorry, but I can't tell you if a member is already here--

GIGI
Dumont, with a T. You tried that?

(*) 3RD BEAT

"UM. DUH. OF COURSE I DID."

FRONT DESK AGENT
I tried it all the ways.

GIGI
(thinks, then)
Small chance he put me under a different name.

"LIAR"

(*) 4th BEAT

FRONT DESK AGENT
Did he.

GIGI
He sometimes puts my birth name on lists, as a bit. It's not funny and has never been funny. It's Jean Dubrowski.

"OF COURSE that's YOUR NAME."

(START TYPING)

FRONT DESK AGENT
I'm going to need you to spell that.

1/2

Figure 2.5. Audition sample sides for a co-star role—with beats and thoughts—page 1.

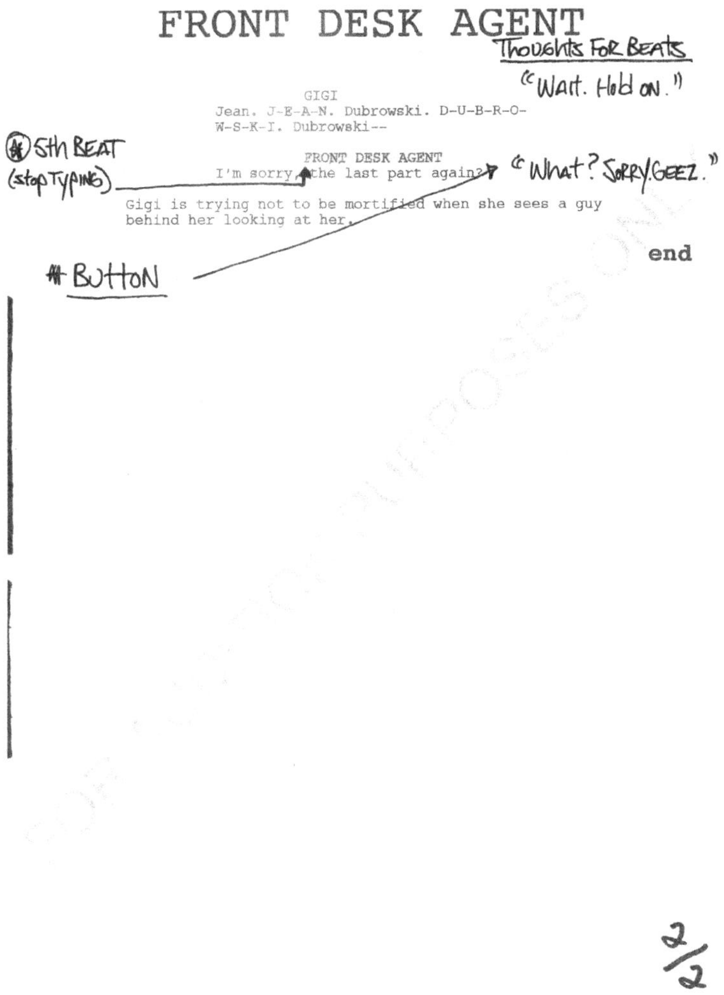

FRONT DESK AGENT

Thoughts for Beats

"Wait. Hold on."

GIGI
Jean. J-E-A-N. Dubrowski. D-U-B-R-O-
W-S-K-I. Dubrowski--

(#) 5th BEAT
(stop typing)

FRONT DESK AGENT
I'm sorry, the last part again? *"What? Sorry. Geez."*

Gigi is trying not to be mortified when she sees a guy
behind her looking at her.

end

- BUTTON

2/2

Figure 2.6. Audition sample sides for a co-star role—with beats and thoughts—page 2.

don't fit well with the character and the given circumstances of the scene.

Actors get so concerned about saying their lines correctly that they frequently take themselves out of the scene, go too fast, and ignore the beats. *Switch your focus to your MAP of beats.* Memorize your MAP and execute it in your audition and your audition will be authentic.

Your Two Most Important Beats: The Need to Speak and the Button

I wanted to go into a bit more detail on these two beats because they are so important. Every on-camera audition needs to have a moment before, or what I call the *need to speak*, and a *button*. Theater auditions can really benefit from these as well, but for on-camera it's critical. And it is surprising how many actors don't use these tools.

Need to Speak

You want your on-camera audition to not look like an audition as much as possible. You just want casting directors and directors to look at your tape and think, "That's the one." If your taped audition begins with you looking directly at your scene partner and saying the first line, it will look like an audition. Why are you speaking? The answer cannot be because you have the first line. Your audition should start with a beat—a moment where something happens that gives you a reason to say your first line. Now sometimes it's the reader who has the first line and you just need to react to them before saying your line. But even if that is the case, when the camera starts rolling, we need something right at the top of the scene to draw casting into what you are thinking, to activate the scene. Here are a couple of technical options to help you:

1. If you have the first line of the scene, create a need to speak: a beat or moment prior to speaking your first line. It could be that you react to an unspoken line the person you are speaking to says. It could be a moment of discovering the person you are speaking to or noticing them for the first time. The beat needs to allow us to see you think and decide to speak. We need to see why you are speaking prior to us hearing your first line.

2. If you do not have the first line, your job is a little easier. You simply need to listen and react to your scene partner's line, which will allow us to see you think and then choose to speak the next line.

In either of these options, a simple, technical, active beat at the top can help draw casting into your scene before you begin. Actors are too eager (and nervous at times) when they start their scenes. Take a beat. Take a breath. Ground yourself.

To be clear: your need to speak should not be a moment where you prepare as an actor. On-camera auditioning is very different from auditioning for the theater. On-camera directors just want you to be the role you are auditioning for, so don't show them how the sausage is made—just be the role. Your need to speak should be a moment that makes sense with what's happening in the scene— not a moment of us watching you prepare as an actor.

That said, always build in a beat at the top where you can take a breath—where you can ground yourself. Make sure that it's not noticeable to a casting director. When I coach actors, I always tell them that auditions can be like speeding trains if you allow them to be. Don't. Because once the speeding train leaves the station, it's almost impossible for you to catch up to it. Your audition will be over, and you'll ask yourself what happened. Flesh out a good, active opening beat with your need to speak, and you'll be able take control of the scene rather than the scene taking control of you.

The Button

Perhaps the most critical beat that your audition must have is the button. Every on-camera audition you do *must* have a button. The button accomplishes two things: (1) it gives your character one last thought, a beat where we can see what you think about the scene that just transpired; and (2) it allows casting to know your audition is over. You'd be surprised at how many self-taped auditions I've watched where actors just stop, don't move, and stare. That is not a button. It can really take casting out of your audition by having them guess, "Is that it? Is there more to the scene?"

Television commercials almost always end in a button, especially if the spot is a comedic one. For example, do an internet search for the 1997 Snickers commercial "Who are the Chefs?" You have a man working at the football stadium for the Kansas City Chiefs. He is shown very carefully painting the name of the team in the endzone. As he stands up, proudly looking at his finished work, a player from the team comes over to him and says, "Hey, that's great. But who are the Chefs?" The player leaves and the voice-over asks, "Not going anywhere for a while?" The man mutters to himself: "Great googly moogly." Then they cut to the product and the voice-over says, "Grab a Snickers." The commercial is over, but there's one more moment that comes after: they show the man, looking at his work, upset with himself, eating a Snickers bar. That same player comes back to him and says, "You spell it…" Before he can finish, the man cuts him off and says, "Ehhh!" That "Ehhh!" is the button.

Television shows have them too. Hour-long television dramas are loaded with them. I'm sure your favorite show has them, so watch some television and look for them. A scene happens between two characters. One of them leaves frame leaving the other character alone—but the camera stays on them. The actor is left having to deliver something that puts a button on the scene before the director shouts, "Cut." It could be a head shake or a sigh—a silent beat where we see a last thought that is active—giving the editor something to cut away from. That is also a button.

Search *Breaking Bad*, the "I am the one who knocks" scene. Bryan Cranston is masterful, but it is Anna Gunn who gets the button of the scene—where we see the impact of Walter White's words and intensity on Skyler's face. Her reaction is a full fifteen seconds after Walter White has left the room, and it's brilliant.

Your on-camera audition needs a button. Here are a few technical tricks to help you land them:

1. *Wherever you were looking for your last line or beat of the scene, simply change where you are looking for the button.* At the end of a two-person scene, take your button to the opposite side of the camera where you ended the scene. This simple change in where you are looking will create a beat change and help put a button on the scene.

2. *Use an intake of breath, a sigh, or even add a word to button the scene.* Using the example above of the Kansas City Chiefs endzone painter, you could add a slight sigh, a breath—or even a single word like "huh" or "Ehhh" for the button. Although your final beat is silent, you are thinking a specific thought. Adding a breath or word can accentuate your final thought.

3. *Don't underestimate what a simple parting of your lips can do.* One of the pioneers of method acting in film and theater, Marlon Brando once said in film, your face is "the proscenium." With that thinking, casting needs to see some kind of change in your face for the button. If your lips are closed at the end of your scene and you then part your lips with a breath for the button, it accentuates a beat change. Nicolas Cage does this beautifully in the classic romantic comedy *Moonstruck* when his character sees Cher for the first time at

the opera. He's looking around for her, lips closed. He sees her, his lips part, and we know instantly that he has seen her and that she has literally taken his breath away.

The goal of the button is to give casting a final thought to see. These three simple, technical tricks look great in the box and allow casting to see that final thought. Don't do an on-camera audition without one.

Your third stop on the roadmap to getting on set has given you everything you need to execute your on-camera audition. Next, we'll take a slight detour and dive into the craft of acting.

CHAPTER THREE

~

A Word (or Two) about Acting 101

Think of this chapter as a slight detour on our roadmap, a chance for you to explore a city on your way to your final destination. Know that you should actually spend a good deal of time in this city—sightseeing and taking in the history—but for purposes of this book and our roadmap, it will be a brief stay.

Most likely, you have received some kind of acting training prior to picking up this book. And although the MAP technique I teach is a technical, on-camera tool that will help you give a great on-camera audition, you really need to know about the craft of acting in order to be successful. That's why the first thing I instruct you to do when you look at your audition sides is to analyze the scene asking three questions. It's very important that you understand the craft of acting.

Analyzing a Scene for Your On-Camera Audition

Being able to pick up a scene and analyze it is essential to auditioning for on-camera—especially if you don't have a lot of time to prepare. If you have time to prepare and are given the whole script for a film or television show you are auditioning for, read the entire script! It's your job to be as prepared as possible. If you are auditioning for a scene on page 10 of the script but learn that your character takes a big turn on page 50, you may be able to plant seeds for that turn or have a deeper understanding of why your character is making the choices they are making on page 10.

If you don't have a lot of time, it's essential that you read the scene and know these three things:

1. Who is my character talking to?
2. What is my relationship to the person I'm talking to?
3. What do I *want from* the person I'm talking to?

The answers to these three questions are important to know for an audition, but perhaps most importantly, you have to know what it is you want from your scene partner. What you want from your scene partner is also called your *objective*.

No matter how new you are to the craft of acting, you should be able to pick up a scene and identify your character's objective. Even if you are auditioning for a cop who has one line, the cop wants something. If it's not obvious on the page, create a want or objective for the character—provided it fits into the world of the story and does not take away from it. Whatever you choose for your objective, remember to keep it active. A passive objective is like not having one at all and can make your on-camera audition one-note.

Why is it important to keep your objective active? Because it keeps the beats in the scene active. An inactive beat is just a pause, and that is not something I encourage actors to take. You must play an objective and your objective should always be active.

Being clear on who you are speaking to and what your relationship is to that person is also critical. It changes the way you read the lines and take the beats. Casting should be able to know with little to no dialogue what your relationship is to the person (or persons) you are speaking to. It helps make your audition that much more authentic. You don't want to give just a general read of the lines. Dig in. Ask these questions and understand your relationships. It will create a sense of history for your character and give your audition that authenticity we are looking for.

Tactics and Obstacles

Understanding scene analysis and playing an objective is important to the arc of the scene. Knowing how to use tactics and obstacles helps give your scene variation, contrast, and different colors. When I'm coaching actors, I frequently try to pull different colors from them, so their auditions have more variety. You want to show casting as much of you as possible. Sometimes you only get a few lines to do so, and sometimes you get a few scenes, but your job in an on-camera audition is always the same—show casting what you are capable of with as much variety as possible.

I spoke about your objective—what you want from your scene partner. Obstacles are what stand in the way of you getting your objective. If you are auditioning for the role of a detective on a television show who is interviewing a suspect, your objective might be "Get my scene partner to tell me the truth." Your obstacle may be that your scene partner is frightened to tell you the truth, perhaps afraid that if they do, their life may be in danger.

You then use different tactics to obtain your objective. In your audition for the detective role, your objective is to get the suspect to tell the truth and your obstacle is they are frightened to tell you. Some tactics you could try include reassuring them, befriending them, or putting them at ease. You may also try putting pressure on them, scaring them, or threatening them. Getting your scene partner to tell you the truth is an active objective, and these tactics will aid in keeping the scene cooking. Whichever tactic you choose is a different color you get to show casting.

Always try to find *contrast* in your choices whenever possible. Contrast is one of the main words I use when I coach actors. You find contrast in your tactics—if you have two scenes you are putting on tape, try to have them be as different as possible, and that lies in the tactics you choose. For our detective, you could choose befriending your scene partner and threatening them. These two different tactics will have a different pace and color to them. Use of different tactics helps create contrast and gives you a more well-rounded audition.

Event of the Scene

Scenes for television and film, especially when you are a co-star, usually have a purpose that helps serve the greater story. In the example I suggested earlier, perhaps you are playing the character of "Joe" on *Chicago PD*. Joe was at the scene of a crime and gets interviewed by Detective Halstead (played by the excellent Jesse Lee Soffer). Joe was able to remember the face of the man who shot his friend. The *event* of the scene may then be this: "Joe gives Detective Halstead a key piece of evidence to help him crack the case."

Understanding the event of the scene helps you do your job as a day player. In the scene you may have a lot of lines, and there may be a lot of intensity or emotion you'll need to bring to it, but your job as the co-star is to help serve the story and the stars of the show (which in this case is Detective Halstead). By the end of the episode, we'll see Halstead solving the case, and your one scene will be key in serving up the story.

Writing out a simple, one-line event of the scene, as we did with the character of Joe, can be helpful for you as an actor. It helps you capture the overall feeling of the scene you are auditioning with and helps you understand your job as the actor in terms of what you need to do to deliver the story. This understanding is especially important when working in television and film—as things move quickly and it really is a *job*.

This book is specifically about on-camera auditioning and learning the new language of on-camera acting. Unfortunately, when it comes to on-camera auditions, we rarely get a chance to look over the copy in a meaningful way. You may have less than twenty-four hours. Do as much as you can—incorporating different tactics and obstacles as outlined in this chapter—but keep in mind what you've learned so far. When you get an on-camera audition, you should have time to do these three things:

1. Analyze the scene asking the three questions mentioned at the start of the chapter: *Who am I talking to? What is my relationship to them? What do I want from them?*
2. Create your MAP of beats that you will use in the scene. Memorize those beats and execute them.
3. Make sure your audition has a need to speak and a button.

If you're able to do just these three things, you will be way ahead of most people auditioning for the same role. You will have confidence and be able to control the audition room rather than it controlling you. You will start to turn those first auditions into callbacks and those callbacks into bookings.

CHAPTER FOUR

Learning the Language
of On-Camera Acting

You now have a blueprint for what to do when you get an on-camera audition. You know how to read the breakdown and analyze your sides with some acting 101 techniques—creating your MAP of beats and having confidence in executing the audition from start to finish. The fourth stop on our roadmap is to make sure that your audition translates in the box. This stop is where you begin to learn the language of on-camera. Again, you can be a brilliant actor, but now you need to deliver your audition through the lens of the camera—and that lens has its own rules. These rules really don't have much to do with acting; they are more about learning a new language and understanding how you look in the box.

In the world of television and film, everything you do happens in the box. There's a great story about the late James Gandolfini referring to it as a box in a book called *10,000 NOs* by Matthew Del Negro. Matthew worked with Mr. Gandolfini on *The Sopranos* and had to do a scene where they were drunk. Mr. Gandolfini starts spinning around to create that drunken feeling and doesn't care if he looks stupid to anyone else on set. He's just trying to give an honest take:

> We did a few takes like this, spinning before each one. And after three or four times through, not because I was really embarrassed, but more in a lame attempt at small talk, I nodded toward the crew and said, "I kinda feel like a jackass spinning like this in front of them." Not one to miss a teaching opportunity, Jim, as we called him, walked over to me and said, "Hey. Don't worry about them." Then he pointed to the matte box that housed the camera and the lens. And in that incredible way that only James Gandolfini could do, he said, "All that matters is that fuckin' box."

That box might be an iPhone, a television monitor, or a movie screen that's thirty feet high. Treat the rules of the box as a technical language you have to learn and speak in order for your acting to resonate. Sometimes, you'll only be able to focus on the technical aspects when you are working: hitting your mark and delivering your line. You will feel like a human prop—and you essentially are. The craft of acting will seem very far away. It's natural to feel that way. You need to shift your mental approach from "showing" to "actively thinking," and once you learn these technical tricks (and many of them are indeed tricks) you will take the pressure off yourself to "show or perform" and you'll be able to just actively think, *be* the character, and let the camera come to you.

Less Is More

This phrase, "less is more" may seem cliché, but what does it really mean and how do you do it? By sometimes literally doing nothing. In addition to incorporating stillness and more economy in your movements, you need to remember this: great on-camera acting is all about watching you think. Well, when it comes to on-camera acting, thinking is really the opposite of showing. You don't need to show anything when it comes to on-camera acting because the camera catches it all. It's a critical adjustment to make if you've only been performing in the theater. But as I've said—it's not about doing nothing. It's about actively thinking and not showing—and that's tough to do. It took me a long time to learn the balance of that lesson.

I was lucky enough to have a director who was also a friend pull me aside and teach me that lesson. I share this anecdote with you in hopes that you learn the "less is more" lesson from this book and *not* on set.

In 2003, I was cast in the role of Kenny in *Employee of the Month*, written by Mitch Rouse and Jay Leggett and directed by Mitch Rouse. It premiered at the Sundance Film Festival in 2004 and has since become a cult classic. Mitch is the husband of my friend Andrea Bendewald, who I went to college with—so I was really given a gift by him putting me in a small role in his movie. The movie starred the likes of Matt Dillon, Steve Zahn, Christina Applegate, and Andrea—not just a friend from college but gifted actor with lots of television credits (such as *Friends* and *Suddenly Susan*), who also taught on-camera acting at UCLA.

We were on set for the big bank robbery scene in the movie. My character is a new employee at the bank—Kenny, whose boss is Matt Dillon. The bank robbers come in and force the employees to get on the floor at gunpoint while they take the money. Andrea and I were together, seated on the floor behind a desk, and Matt Dillon was across from us. In the scene, Matt tries to get Andrea to push the alarm button under the desk, which my character thinks is a terrible idea. There's no dialogue, just a look between Matt, Andrea, and me. On action, although just sitting on the floor, I would use my face, and even my hands, to show the camera that I was thinking the line "Don't push the alarm button!"

Mitch yells, "Action!" and we do the scene. We hear "Cut!" and Mitch comes over to Andrea and me:

Mitch: "Hey. You guys can bring it down and do a little less."

Stef and Andrea: "Ok, cool. No problem."

Mitch yells, "Action!" and we go again—doing much less (we think). We hear "Cut!" Andrea and I turn to each other and say, "Well, that felt great. You were awesome!" while patting each other on the back.

Mitch comes over to us again.

Mitch: "Guys. You can bring it down more. It's still too big."

Stef and Andrea: "Really? Wow. We thought that one felt good. But, of course. You got it."

We go again. This time, I'm looking over at Matt Dillon and, from where I'm sitting, I'm thinking, "Well, Matt's not doing anything. I need do something more than what he's doing." I still had the mentality that I needed to "show" in order to execute my objective. But I take Mitch's direction (I think) and finish the take.

Mitch yells "Cut!" This time he stops us and says, "Ok, guys. Come take a look at something with me." He brings us over to the monitor and very generously (while Matt and the crew are waiting) shows us the take of our closeup. Then he shows us Matt's closeup.

I looked like I was doing a production of *Oklahoma!* on Broadway—full on mugging with my face, using big gestures with my hands, and "showing" everyone—including the camera, "DON'T PUSH THE ALARM BUTTON!" It was as if I were playing to the back row of a theater. While Matt, without doing anything except using his eyes, conveys the stakes and objective of the scene perfectly in two seconds because he has been acting on film since he was a teenager. He has had the benefit of years of experience and reps in front of the camera. He is a pro.

Andrea told me later that when watching Matt, it was as if she could see him thinking in that moment—he was that clear with his thoughts. That's exactly right. She also remembered Mitch telling us, "Guys. You have to understand that your faces are going to be on a screen that is thirty feet high. Anything you do in this shot will look huge. That's why you need to bring it way down."

I was extremely lucky to have Mitch take the time to teach me the lesson of "less is more" and save me from embarrassment. Most of you will not be as lucky, and you'll need to know this lesson for your on-camera auditions as well as when you book the job.

I shot this movie long before I learned that on-camera acting is really a different language that at times has nothing to do with the craft of acting I studied in school. I did a couple of independent and short films after I worked with Mitch, but it took me a while to learn the lesson that *less* really is *more*, and it's about thinking and not showing. If thinking and not showing is key to great on-camera acting, then use of the MAP will help you flesh out and nail silent acting beats such as the one I failed to do for Mitch in *Employee of the Month*.

Theater Acting versus On-Camera Acting

In theater, directors are looking for good actors—actors will spend two to four weeks creating the world of a play or musical. Then there are tech rehearsals, previews, and the actual run of the show. There's something about auditioning for theater—where your abilities as an actor are on display a bit more. When you are working with a director at a callback for theater, they want to see your actor muscles and know that you are directable. After all, you're going to be spending weeks together creating the world of a play.

When auditioning for television and film, there's no time for that. You just need to show up on set ready to go. Often when you do a television or film job, you won't even be directed at all.

On-camera directors don't want actors, especially for co-stars. You may have heard the expression "Plays are performed. Movies are made." This is the absolute truth. Television and film directors don't have time to watch you craft a character (or walk you over to the monitor to show you how big you are being on screen). They need you to be the person you are auditioning for, show up, and do the job. Having an actor who needs special time and care costs producers time and money they don't have on a set. Walk in the room and be the person you are auditioning for. It's as simple as that.

Playing with "Less Is More" to the Extreme

As we continue on our roadmap, think of this story as another detour to enrich your understanding of how simply doing "less is more," even to the extreme, can help you with your on-camera audition.

I auditioned for the pilot for the Fox television show *Empire*. The role was a record executive with one line: "Can you give me something more like Color Me Bad?" I was auditioning for the show's creator, Lee Daniels. I remember sitting in the waiting room at the casting director's office. Every time an actor would come out of the audition room, the casting director would come out and say, "Guys: you're all being too big. You need to bring it way down. If you think you're being small, you can do even less. He's getting really frustrated." Well, after hearing that news I thought, "What do I have to lose?" I decided to go in there and do absolutely nothing and try a purely technical reading as an experiment (as I probably wasn't going to book this job anyway).

I walked into the audition room and Mr. Daniels was seated on the couch. He looked at my résumé and said, "Hey, Stef. I'd get up and shake your hand, but if I have to shake one more actor's hand, I'm going to throw up." I'm completely serious. That's what he said to me *before* I had to do my audition! So, I said, "Ok then." I sat down in the chair, took my time, and did what I thought was nothing.

It was a ridiculous read when I think back on it. I took a beat, scratched my face, looked around, and broke up the line—"Can you give me something more like Color Me Bad?"—reading it in a barely audible voice. When I finished, Mr. Daniels stood up, walked over to me, shook my hand, and said, "Now *that* was worth getting up for. THANK YOU." I was put on hold for the role before I even got back to my car. (The role was eventually cut from the pilot, so I ended up not booking the pilot anyway. I wound up doing an episode of *Empire* years later though.)

I tell this story to illustrate a point: by doing less and employing a few simple, technical tricks that I will teach you in the next chapter, I was able to make an award-winning director stand up and shake my hand. But don't misunderstand me: Analyze the scene. Create your MAP of beats. Prepare. But in addition to these things, you need to learn the language of on-camera acting and use it to your advantage.

CHAPTER FIVE

~

Technical Tricks to Help You Speak the Language of On-Camera Acting

Everything you do for your on-camera audition all happens in a box. Whether you go into a casting director's office, do a virtual callback, or submit a self-tape on your own, your audition is being looked at in a box. It could be a thirty-two-inch television monitor that the casting director is seeing you on, an iPhone that the director (who is on set shooting something else) is looking at, or a computer screen where they are watching your self-tape or virtual callback. That's what you've got to work with. Even if the casting director or director is present in the room for your audition, 99 percent of the time they will be watching you on the monitor and not looking at you in the room. After all, they need to see how you will look in the "box" where their audience will be watching you.

It's on our fifth stop of our roadmap where you will learn technical tricks to help you speak the language of on-camera acting. But before you learn these tricks, you need to learn how to look your best in the box.

The focus of an on-camera audition should always be on your eyes. If you go into a casting director's office to do your on-camera audition, generally you will be given a mark on the floor—an X that will be between your feet. You will have someone reading the scene with you—they may be seated in front of you, standing next to the camera—or they may be running the camera at the same time they are reading with you.

In the frame, you will be elbows up, and there should be just a little space between the top of your head and the top of the frame (see figures 5.1 and 5.2). Even if you are submitting a self-tape for a theater job, you want the focus to always be your eyes and the frame should be the same.

This means that you don't need a lot of movement. Are you restricted in your movement? Well, no. You can move as you would when doing the action of the scene—as long as you stay on your mark and in your frame. Unlike a theater audition on a stage, you

Figure 5.1. Example of an actor (Terry Bell) in correct on-camera audition frame. Brandon Dahlquist Photography.

Figure 5.2. **Example of an actor (Rochelle Therrien) in correct on-camera audition frame. Brandon Dahlquist Photography.**

cannot move from your mark, roam around, and expect whoever is running the camera in the audition to follow you. Stay on your mark and deliver the scene. Remember: it's all about watching you think when it comes to an on-camera audition. Whether you are auditioning for a job in theater or television and film, if we are watching your audition in the box, the rules of the box will always apply. And stillness can be golden in the box.

The language of on-camera is very technical. I refer to the four techniques covered here as "tricks" because they are to be applied to your acting skill set, but they really have nothing to do with the craft of acting. It actually requires you to unlearn some of what you have learned in acting school to be effective.

Eye Locking and the "Thinking Places"

Why is the shot so tight when you audition on-camera? Well, as I've said, it's because on-camera acting is all about watching you *think*—and that happens with your eyes. In the box, your eyes tell the story. If you watch any television show or movie, watch the actor's eyes. Where they look tells you where the story is unfolding. For your audition, it is critical that the focus is on your eyes, that your eyes are well lit, and that you understand where to look when the camera is rolling.

Many actors that I've coached over the years have a habit of looking their scene partner directly in the eye, staying with them and not looking away 100 percent of the time. It's a way of showing that you are a good scene partner; you are listening and staying connected to them. That's not actually what we do in real life when talking with someone, and it doesn't work for on-camera acting. When you audition for an on-camera job, we are only seeing *you* in the box, not your scene partner. And many times, when you are auditioning, you won't be able to physically *see* your scene partner. The focus is always on you—even if you are auditioning in person, you will most likely be reading with someone who is not an actor—just a reader. Being a good scene partner for your on-camera audition is not important.

If good on-camera acting is about watching you think, we need to see the thoughts hit your brain. Eye-locking on a scene partner when you are auditioning for an on-camera role will not help the casting director or director see your thoughts. If you just stay with your reader for your entire scene, your audition will look very one-note in the box (see figure 5.3).

Your scene partner is your focus for sure, but how can we allow casting to watch us think? By using a tool I call the *thinking places.*

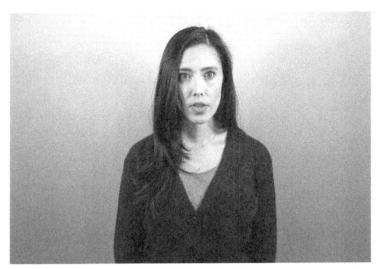

Figure 5.3. Example of an eye-locked actor (Rochelle Therrien). Brandon Dahlquist Photography.

The thinking places will vary depending on whether you are shooting a self-tape at home, auditioning at a casting director's office, virtually over Zoom, or actually being on set. But generally, put your thinking places to the right or left of your scene partner's eyes, making sure to keep your eyes up and not look at the floor. I've included an image of a basic, at home self-tape set up with a smartphone, and where the thinking places are in conjunction with your "sweet spot." The sweet spot on a smart phone is where you should place your main scene partner, and it's a bit closer to the lens of the camera than you think. It's where your eyes will look best in the box, yet still feel like you are talking to your main scene partner without looking directly into the lens of the camera—which you should never do (see figure 5.4).

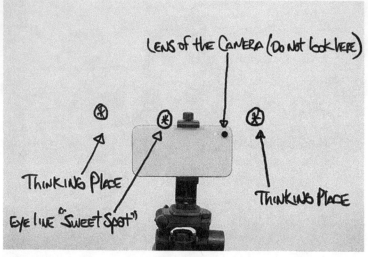

Figure 5.4. Here we see what you will be looking at when you self-tape your audition. Note the "sweet spot" for your eye line as well as your Thinking Places. **Brandon Dahlquist Photography.**

Take the following line of dialogue:

JOANNE

She'd been doing so well . . . when she told me she was stopping, I just, I had to do something. Dr. please, you remember her hallucinations, how bad it got. You can't say anything. I'm only trying to protect her. I'm begging you. Please.

If the actor gives the previous line of dialogue straight to her scene partner and never looks away, you won't see the thoughts hit her brain. It will seem as though she is just reciting a line she has memorized, and she will look eye locked. But if she breaks up the line, perhaps using a beat and one or both of the thinking places as she is forming her thoughts, it looks as if she is choosing her words and coming up with the line for the very first time. The actor gets the thought—or finds the words she's trying to say—in the thinking place and then shares her thoughts and words with her scene partner (see figures 5.5 and 5.6).

It's a very simple technique, but you'd be amazed at how few actors actually have an understanding of it and how much it helps them look natural and authentic in the box. It also works when you have to do a monologue for a theater audition. Eye locking makes the monologue feel too rehearsed and less like a scene—which is how a monologue should feel.

So, when you set up the room for an on-camera audition—either at a casting director's office or for an in-home self-tape, you should clock where the camera is, where your scene partner is

Figure 5.5. Actor using the Thinking Place—moving their eyes to the Thinking Place to get the thought. Brandon Dahlquist Photography, Rochelle Therrien, Actor.

Figure 5.6. Actor using the Thinking Place—moving their eyes back to their scene partner to share their thought with their next line. Brandon Dahlquist Photography, Rochelle Therrien, Actor.

(again, usually the casting director or intern reading with you— not an actor) and choose two thinking places, one on either side of your scene partner. Use them (see figures 5.5 and 5.6 above). Your focus will still be your scene partner (the casting director or reader), but use the thinking places to find your thoughts and choose your words—this will allow casting to see your thoughts. If your character is recalling a memory in your audition scene, use the thinking places to see the memory first and then describe it. This allows casting (and the audience) to see it as well. You allow casting and the audience to see your thoughts by using the thinking places—not by eye-locking with your scene partner.

If you're looking for a perfect example of an actor using the thinking place in an actual film and not just an audition, watch Viola Davis as Suzy Brown opposite the late Chadwick Boseman's James Brown in *Get On Up*. In the third act of the film, watch when Suzy and James reunite and she says, "I left—because I loved you." She's stunning (as always) and when her eyes move off of Chadwick to the thinking place, we see her pain and the history of her character by Viola simply moving her eyeline away from her scene partner.

Vertical Eye Movement

Something else that can help you look better in the box is vertical eye movement. You'd be surprised at how good using vertical (or up and down) eye movement makes you look in the box. Particularly if your relationship to your scene partner is that of a love interest. It will give your audition variation, contrast, and give your relationship to your scene partner more clarity.

An example of simple, vertical eye movement can be found in the Progressive Insurance commercial "Group Outing." Sixteen seconds in you see Dr. Rick say, "Garth, did he ask for your help?" Garth takes a wonderful beat to think about it, says "No," then looks at the person he was talking to up and down with vertical eye movement. He then says "No" again. It's a great button mid-scene, helped with vertical eye movement. If the actor playing Garth just stayed with his scene partner and looked him directly in the eyes, the moment would not have had the same impact.

All this is to say: keep your eyes up! No matter if you use the thinking places or vertical eye movement, you cannot allow people to watch your character think if you are looking down at the floor—or even close to it. Keep your eyes up at all times. Even if your character is sitting down and slumped, look up toward the camera with those eyes and let the camera do the work of watching you think.

Volume

The volume with which you speak your lines on-camera is the complete opposite of theater and what you were taught in your undergrad acting program. When you walk on a television or film set, one of the first things you'll notice when you start working with the other actors is this: you can't hear them. That's not an exaggeration. You sometimes literally cannot hear them speak the lines that you are supposed to be listening and reacting to. Why is that? Well in television and film, in addition to a boom mic (a microphone on a long pole that someone is holding over you as you speak your lines), usually if you speak any lines at all, you most definitely are wearing a microphone. That microphone is so small that it fits under your collar, in the knot of your tie, or in your blouse. And it picks up everything, every sound and every breath. There's no need to project on set. In fact, you should do the opposite. Watch any television show, even the ones taped in front of a live audience, and you'll notice almost all of the characters use a whispered tone when they are speaking. Knowing how to use the microphone and modulate your voice for television and film is paramount, and it starts with learning how to modulate your voice in your audition.

Again: keep in mind they don't want to hire an actor for an on-camera job—they want you to be the character. They don't want to see your training. When you have lines to speak, the lower your volume, the more natural you sound—and less like an actor.

Breaking Up a Line and Making It Your Own

Every actor works differently, but many television and film actors choose to not look at their lines until they get on set. Many times, they show up and go over their lines for the day in the makeup trailer. They do this because they want their dialogue to sound natural. You will hear this when working on-camera all the time. My favorite is when a director says to you, "That's great. Now just throw it away more." Throw it away? What on earth do they mean? What they mean is that you are delivering the line like an actor, not a real person; you are too big, or you are enunciating too much and perhaps too loudly. Also, the line itself may be a bit clunky and throwing it away might make it sound more natural; more on that below.

Again, in television and film, they don't want actors. They just want you to be the person you are portraying. They don't have time to watch your process. They need you to show up, hit your mark, and deliver the lines—rehearsed and ready to go, natural and believable. So how do you do that and memorize and prepare for a role the way you learned in school or from your experience of working in the theater?

A Word about Dialogue for Television and Film

There are some excellent television and film scripts out there, but much of the dialogue you will say—especially in your television auditions where they sometimes use "dummy scripts," scripts that are used strictly for auditions and not for shooting—won't be good. You can tell when you have to deliver dialogue that is clunky or melodramatic. There are many reasons for this: first and foremost, the pace of producing television is incredibly fast. It's expensive and there isn't time for weeks of rehearsals and previews to perfect the dialogue. Quite often, the first time dialogue gets said outside of the writer's room is in an audition or on set. Remember: plays are performed; television and films are made.

In theater, we are taught to read the lines as written. The playwright is revered in the rehearsal process and you never change a single word of dialogue without it coming from the playwright. For television and film, it's much different. Lots of times actors are told to "make the dialogue their own" or add or subtract words last minute. The dialogue is more fluid and, depending on the set, writers are just another part of the crew. I remember my first episode of *Chicago Fire* (Season 1). I had a question about my character, Daniel Schwartz. I knew he had money, but I didn't know what he did for a living. Was he in finance? A lawyer? So naturally, having a background in theater, I sought out the writer. It took me a bit to find her, and when I approached her, she seemed shocked (and pleasantly surprised) that I had a question for her. After a brief discussion, she thought that my character was a lawyer and that informed the scene for me.

I mention this story to point out that the writer on a television set might not be available or have time for twenty questions with you—especially if you are a co-star. You're going to have to figure out most things on your own and go with them—perhaps to be given a note later by the director. It's on you, the actor, to deliver great dialogue naturally and make lesser dialogue sound great.

So how do we make dialogue that is clunky or melodramatic— or even good dialogue for that matter—sound "natural"? The first thing is to learn to break dialogue up and not make it sound so "clean." I use the word clean to illustrate the difference between speaking dialogue in the theater as opposed to television and film. There is a certain cleanliness to saying lines from an Arthur Miller play, and sometimes actors love to chew on the words instead of throwing them away. Let's take our previous example:

JOANNE

She'd been doing so well . . . when she told me she was stopping, I just, I had to do something. Dr. please, you remember her hallucinations, how bad it got. You can't say anything. I'm only trying to protect her. I'm begging you. Please.

Try reading this line out loud cleanly. Meaning, exactly as written without any beats or breaking up the line. Might sound a bit clunky or melodramatic. But if you break it up, and as I've suggested, use beats and thinking places to search for and choose the words you are saying, it may look more like this:

JOANNE

She'd been doing so well . . . when she told me she was **(BEAT)** stopping, I just—I had to do something.

(BEAT)

Dr. **(BEAT)** please—you remember her hallucinations— how **(BEAT)** bad it got. You can't say anything. I'm only trying to protect her. I'm begging you. **(BEAT)** Please.

The acting 101 approach to the beats I'm illustrating here is the character thinking of what to say to the doctor in order for her to achieve her objective—but by simply breaking up the dialogue in a technical way, it helps the dialogue sound more natural. In the frame of the shot, using the "thinking places" to search for the right word to say to the doctor, we see the character struggling and working out how to get what she wants in the scene. Lastly, modulating your voice to a quiet whisper at times will make the dialogue sound more real.

By doing these three technical things:

1. Breaking up the dialogue with small beats
2. Using the "thinking places" to choose the words and see your thoughts
3. Modulating your voice to an appropriate level for on-camera (which could even be a whisper)

We achieve these goals:

1. Making the dialogue sound more natural
2. Allowing the audience to watch the character think
3. Fooling the audience into thinking that we are coming up with these words in the moment

It's really a matter of putting aside some good habits we may have learned as trained theater actors:

1. Look directly in the eyes of your scene partner and stay with them.
2. Memorize your lines inside and out, and deliver them cleanly.
3. Use a trained, projected voice when speaking on stage, so you can be heard in the back row of the theater.

A great example of these technical "tricks" married together with great acting can be seen in the television show *Mad Men*. Search for "Don Draper fires Lane Pryce." Both actors give amazing performances in this scene, but Jon Hamm's breaking up of the dialogue, voice modulation, and even use of thinking places when trying to decide what to do about Lane illustrate exactly my point when it comes to applying these three technical tricks.

Having Multiple Scene Partners

Having multiple scene partners in an on-camera audition can be tricky and there are different thoughts on how to handle it. My view is to set up the scene using different focus points for each character you are speaking to. Use the off-camera reader as the character you are speaking to the most and place the other characters in proximity to the reader—addressing them individually as if you were reading the scene with several people instead of just one.

If you are doing a scene with a group of friends—let's say Tom, Dick, and Harry—and Tom is the character who you are speaking to the most, then Tom would be the reader. Place Dick and Harry on the opposite side of the camera from Tom. Now it's tricky because you've really have to know the scene. The reader will be reading all of Tom, Dick, and Harry's lines; and you've got to know when each is speaking so you can change your eye focus.

I like this way of doing multiple character scenes for auditions because it gives casting more to see from you—different angles, contrast—rather than looking in one spot the entire take. This slight variation gives your audition something extra to take note of rather than just a straight read in one direction.

Eye contact with the reader is important—you always want to stay with them if you can. But if they are looking down a lot or seated and you are standing, make sure you don't get caught with your head and eyes angled down for your entire audition. If that happens, simply focus just above the reader's eyes—perhaps at their forehead—to make sure you keep your head up and stay in correct frame.

Environment

A sense of environment is created when you have multiple characters in a scene. That environment is a much different room than when you are doing a one-on-one scene. Actors take environment for granted when auditioning on-camera, but if you can incorporate a sense of environment, using multiple scene partners or just on your own, it can make your audition really pop. Here are some tips for incorporating a sense of environment in your on-camera audition:

1. In addition to using the thinking places, when doing a two-person scene (or even a multiple person scene), create a sense of environment by clocking your surroundings. Where does the scene take place? Coffee shop? Hospital room? You can't play your surroundings, but you can clock them. Modulate your voice depending on where you are. If the scene takes place in a restaurant, you may lower your voice so the

table next to you doesn't hear you. Same with a hospital room—perhaps there is someone on the other side of the room (behind a curtain). If you are in a locker room or at a club, your voice may be a bit louder.

2. If you have multiple people in the scene, your relationship with each character should be slightly different. How you speak to your mother is different from how you speak to a love interest or a sibling. Make sure you have an awareness of your relationship to each character and how they are different. Again—finding contrast.

3. Lastly, if you are doing a self-tape and not auditioning at a casting director's office, try not to use the standard, dark-blue background most casting offices use. It immediately showcases that you are giving an audition. It's tough to bring authenticity and a sense of environment when the background looks like every other audition casting will watch. If you can, find another option—gray or even a light green. Whatever you choose to wear for the character, make sure the colors pop with the backdrop.

All of these things can give your on-camera audition a sense of environment and make it feel authentic—instead of feeling like just an audition. As I've said and now shown, it really is a different language to which you are applying your acting skills. Once you understand the rules of the box and how it works, you can apply these technical "tricks" to your on-camera audition. It will make your performance land in a way that was not possible without them. This was an important stop on our roadmap to getting on set: understanding the technical rules of the box, using technical tricks to help you speak the language of on-camera so you can focus on your MAP of beats, and taking your time in your audition. More on that in the next chapter.

CHAPTER SIX

~

Auditioning in Person

*A Word about Casting Directors,
Audition Rooms, and Nerves*

Our next stop is one that few actors enjoy and most dread: auditioning in person for a casting director. The job of a casting director is tough, and what you think may be going on behind the scenes and the reasons why you do or don't get called in for roles most likely aren't what you think.

You need to focus on the thing you can control: your preparation. That's really all you can control. The audition room, the mood of the casting director (or director if you get a callback), if they are behind, if your reader has never read the scene before, the placement of the camera in the room, if it's raining outside—you get the idea. You cannot control any of these things, and you must learn to accept that and be flexible.

Every casting director and director is different, but to be safe, here's what *you can expect* in the room for your on-camera audition at a casting director's office:

1. Expect not to be given any direction
2. Expect not to be told a synopsis of the script or what is happening in your particular scene

3. Expect that sometimes, when you have prepared four scenes, they will only ask for one, and you'll have to choose which one on the spot
4. Expect not to be told if you should sit or stand for your audition
5. Expect that you may want to take some of these things personally

I know how you feel! We are actors, and we long for validation. We want direction. However, that's just not how the world of on-camera works. This is not to say that casting directors don't want you to succeed. It's just that most of the time (certainly not all of the time) things are moving very quickly, and there simply isn't time to have your hand held and be walked through your audition. And you will be nervous! Of course you will, because you are a human being and not a robot. So how do you calm yourself and not give in to nerves?

The good news is when you book the job and get on set—it's worse.

What can you do to execute your on-camera audition and not let the room or casting director own you? How do you not let your nerves take over? Keep it simple. Focus on these three things, which will help you tremendously:

Set the Room

Setting the room is key. Once you walk in and say a brief hello, check out the room. Clock where the camera is. Clock where your scene partner or reader will be. Clock your thinking places in relation to the camera. If you are speaking to more than one person in the scene, place them. Use things in the room (a light, a picture on the wall, etc.) as placeholders for the other characters, if that's helpful.

If there is a chair and you want to use it, use it. If you'd like a chair to sit in and you don't see one, politely ask for one. Take a second to set up the room so that you can do your job. Focus on your MAP!

Take Your Time

I know this might be a taboo thing to say, but it's true: TAKE. YOUR. TIME. As I said when I showed you how to create your MAP of beats, always find a beat to take at the very top of the scene—maybe two. One in the need to speak and one shortly thereafter. If you don't find a beat to take at the top, your audition will begin like that speeding train leaving the station, and you will not be able to catch up to it.

Do not take a pause at the top where we see you the actor preparing—taking a big deep breath, closing your eyes, cracking your neck, or doing some sort of vocal exercise. Please do not do that. Remember: casting does not want to see an actor. They want to see a human. They want to see the person perfect for the role, so just be it. They do not want to watch how you get there.

Just focus on your MAP of beats and take them. Nail them. Don't rush through them. It may be the number one thing I see when I coach actors: they rush. They do not trust themselves to allow the camera to come to them. They think that if they take a beat and don't come right in with their next line, they will lose the people watching their audition. The result is they rush through their audition, and it's over in thirty seconds.

When actor Robin Wright was directing *House of Cards* for the first time, she went to director David Fincher for advice and he told her, "Think of a fraction and put the word 'behavior' on the top of the line and the word 'time' underneath, so it's behavior over time. That's all you need to remember." Behavior in television and film is about watching you think and process. It's watching behavior, not reciting lines.

You are in the audition room (or submitting a self-tape) because casting wants to see you. You've earned the right to take your time. Take it. I mean this. I've had agents (not casting directors, interestingly) fight me on this. It is absolutely ok to take your time as long as you are active. I've had agents who've said, "Yeah, just tighten it up" or "Pick up the pace." Here's the thing: pace in television and film is dictated by the editor, not the actor. If you blow through a scene quickly because you think you need to pick up the pace, you are doing a disservice not only to your performance but to the editor whose job it is to cut the scenes together to make the story. Give them something to work with. Take. Your. Time.

Smile

I know this may sound corny, but it works. Do it—even if the scene is a serious one. Smile ever so slightly to yourself before you start. And breathe. Things are always easier to do when you breathe and smile.

I was auditioning for a play at Steppenwolf Theatre Company, directed by *Chicago PD* regular and Tony-nominated actress Amy Morton. I saw Amy Morton on stage when I was in college in a play called *Once in Doubt* at the now defunct Remains Theatre in Chicago with William Petersen and Gerry Becker. I loved her and followed her theater and television and film career over the years; I was a huge fan and nervous to audition for her. I got the script for the play with just two days to prepare for the audition. It was a lot of work. Two completely different characters, and one of the characters I was reading for was a seventy-year-old woman.

When I went in the audition room, it was packed. Two readers, the playwright, casting director, a camera, about four other people, and, of course, Amy. And she could not have been nicer. She introduced herself (as if I or anyone else didn't know who she was!) and asked if I had any questions before I jumped in. I was so tense, nervous, and focused that I let the room completely take control of me. She had opened a door—I could have very easily said, "Actually yes. I read the script but only got it a couple days ago. There's a lot here to dig into. In terms of the physicality, is there a baseline for you? I'm assuming keep it simple?" I'm not saying you should always ask questions before you start or that my question examples are correct, but if the director or casting director opens a door for you, gingerly walk through it.

But I didn't. I got super serious and started the scene, only to be stopped three lines in by Amy. She was trying to help me, but I let the room control me and got too nervous to execute the scene and do my work. I was too nervous to listen and be present. What I should have done was taken a breath—and smiled. I've got Amy Morton here working with me! Let's work together on this— breathe, Stef. I didn't let that happen, and I didn't do my best work.

Smile in the room—if only to yourself (not for casting to see). You're getting the opportunity to show your work. You've earned the right to be there. Find a way to enjoy the moment.

Don't Take It Personally

This might be the hardest thing to do, but you've got to walk in and out of these audition rooms without taking anything that happens personally. It's a job, and most of the time when you audition you are in and out, and you won't have a sense of how the audition went. For as many auditions you go on feeling that way, there will be times where you'll feel great about the work you did, where you have ample time to prepare, where you get excellent direction, and where casting takes their time with you and makes you feel really good about your work.

However, the only thing you can truly count on is *you*. Prepare as best you can and set the room, take your time and smile, be proud of your work and leave it at the door—because everything else is out of your control.

A Quick Word about Wardrobe and Props

Students always ask me if they can use props in their auditions. The answer is always the same: no. Why? Because great on-camera acting and auditioning is about watching you think, not use props. There are of course exceptions, but the general rule is this: unless it's a cell phone—or if you are drinking in a scene, a water bottle perhaps (scenes where you are drinking something look way better with an actual drink)—a purse, or your sides that you hold in your audition, don't use props.

When it comes to wardrobe for an audition—you want to dress to character, but not in full costume. Read the breakdown. If your character is a lawyer, you might want to wear something more formal depending on the given circumstances of the scene. However, if you are auditioning for a doctor, you do not need to wear scrubs or a lab coat. And don't go out and buy clothes for an audition—save your money. You are elbows to the top of your head with a focus on your eyes. Same with facial hair, makeup, and glasses. You don't want to wear anything that might detract from your performance.

CHAPTER SEVEN

~

Sending in a Self-Tape Audition
Stef's Dos and Don'ts

This is a critical stop on your roadmap to being on set. More than ever, casting is accepting self-tapes as a way of auditioning for roles for both theater and on-camera jobs. I've seen actors book leading roles for theater off a self-tape alone. I booked an episode of the short-lived CBS show *Proven Innocent* and Showtime's *The Chi* (in co-star roles) off a self-tape. The best part of auditioning with a self-tape? You truly get to control every aspect of your audition. From the audition room to the take itself, you control 100 percent of the process. Also, gone are the days where we only had four networks producing television—CBS, NBC, ABC, and FOX. With Netflix, Amazon, HBO, Showtime, Starz, and countless others, there are a number of studios creating content on various platforms, more than ever before. The opportunities for actors to book work and be seen by self-tapes has never been greater.

If you are able, always send in a self-tape. Why? Because wouldn't you rather have 100 percent control of every aspect of your audition? Yes, you would. As an actor just breaking into the business, you must learn how to create a professional self-tape that will book you jobs. And by that, I mean your self-tape must be of a quality that a television or film director will watch it and think, "That's the actor I'm looking for." Think of your self-tapes as being a short film where you are the director, producer, and star. Your short film should have a beginning, middle, and end. Your self-tape should look great not only on a large television monitor but on a computer screen or a smartphone as well. Remember, sometimes directors are on set when they look at your self-tape. They might be watching your tape from their smartphone while in between takes shooting something else. The good news is that, if you are self-taping your audition on a decent smartphone (like an iPhone 8 or newer) it has a camera built in that is far superior to many of the camcorders you see in casting director's offices, and the quality should be fine for viewing.

Sometimes, your agent will have you come in and tape your audition at their office. In Chicago, Los Angeles, New York, and Atlanta, there are plenty of studios where you can go in and have someone professionally do your self-tape for you for anywhere from $50 to $150. But more than ever, inexpensive equipment is available for you to purchase and do self-tapes in the comfort of your own home. I highly recommend it.

You can shoot takes on an iPhone with a good need to speak and button and not need to edit your takes. Or you can put your takes into iMovie and edit them before sending. You can then send the takes using WeTransfer (also known as "Collect" by WeTransfer—available for both iOS and Android phones) right from the iPhone to your agent or directly to the casting director. You can also upload your takes right from your phone to Actors Access using the "Ecocast" portal. Check out actorsaccess.com.

I purchased my first in-home set up on Amazon in 2017. It included a light green backdrop, a tripod, a front box light, and two LED lights to assist with shadows on the backdrop (see figure 7.1). Everything cost me around $175.

Figure 7.1. **Example of an in-home self-tape set up using a box light with side lighting. Brandon Dahlquist Photography**

I know ring lights have become popular as well, but ring lights tend to give actors a donut white ring around the iris of their eyes that more and more directors and casting directors do not like. However, you can simply turn the ring light around, turn the power up to full, and reflect it off another surface—a white wall, white cardboard, or a bounce card. This is especially helpful if you want to do a self-tape while wearing glasses, so you don't get a harsh glare in your lens.

I've also seen actors who are on the road in a hotel room do self-tapes with a painting clip light, make-shift tripod, and their phones. You can use dryer sheets or wax paper to soften the light. The technology today is even better and less expensive than what I bought years ago.

In addition to your self-tape equipment, you'll need access to a printer—both to print out your sides (I would avoid using your smart phone or tablet to hold your audition sides while filming) and to sign the occasional NDA to submit with your audition. Many projects require a signed NDA, or non-disclosure agreement, so that details for the project are not leaked to the public.

Everyone will do what they can when it comes to an in-home set up. I've coached actors who have three small children running around while trying to self-tape an audition, actors who live in studio apartments and have no room for lights, and actors that couldn't afford the equipment right away. I will tell you what I tell them—do what you can; however, it is in your best interest to invest and make sure your in-home set up is a good one. Self-tapes are going to be the way actors get jobs for a very long time, and anything you can do to make your self-tapes look like well-produced short films is going to help your chances. You don't want to give casting anything that takes away from your eyes or performance, so good lighting and a backdrop are imperative at the least. Again, see the photos in chapter 5 on what a perfect frame (well lit, clear background, elbows to top of your head) should look like.

The information I am giving you on self-tapes I have gathered from workshops I've taken at SAG-AFTRA offices, breakdowns I've seen that detail what exactly casting directors want from your self-tape, and feedback I've received from casting directors and agents. *But . . .* when you are doing a self-tape, make sure you read the breakdown and look at what the casting directors are asking of you! Every casting director is different, and they may be asking for something slightly different from what I am laying out for you here.

Here are my dos and don'ts for in-home self-tapes:

DO:

- Tape indoors if possible: to control lighting/sound.
- Use a tripod or something to set your camera or phone on. If your camera is handheld for your take, casting won't even watch it.

- Always shoot horizontally. Casting won't watch your tape if it is shot vertically.
- Keep the camera at eye level or slightly above. Make sure it's not too low, where we are seeing your nostrils.
- Frame should be close—your elbows to top of your head with a slight space between your head and top of frame. Focus is always on your eyes.
- Make sure that you are in focus and well-lit. Both eyes should be visible and present.
- Have the background be uncluttered with no visual noise. Many casting offices use a brighter blue background. I prefer medium to light gray. Try to not make it look like an audition tape. If you hang a sheet for your background, make sure there are no wrinkles—they can be distracting. Keep the background clean.
- When lighting, eliminate shadows if possible. Cast the light down on your face from above; aim lights at the center of your nose.
- Make sure you use a reader! Someone off camera who is reading the other lines of the scene. It will be difficult for casting to take your tape seriously without it. They can also assist in turning the camera on and off (there are also Bluetooth remotes available to start and stop recording on your phone so you can do it yourself.) If you are on the road with a show, on vacation, or in the middle of the desert and you absolutely cannot find anyone to be a reader for you, you can try recording the other characters' lines ahead of time (the LineLearner app, available for both iOS and Android devices, is a good way to do this)—or try to Skype, Zoom, or FaceTime someone in. Desperate times call for desperate measures.
- When using a reader, make sure they speak quietly as they will be next to the camera, and the microphone will pick up their voice over yours. Also—avoid having the reader

"act" with you. Just have them read the lines with a flat read. You should never be upstaged by the reader. It's distracting. Watch for big volume changes, mouth noise, and breathing sounds.

DO NOT:

- Do not look directly in the lens. Have your reader stand just off camera. If you are using a smart phone, please note the "sweet spot" shown in the photo in chapter 5 (figure 5.4), as well as your thinking places.
- Do not have someone hold the camera for your take. Use a tripod or set the camera on something.
- Do not wear colors that are too bright or have a lot of patterns or visual noise.
- Do not wear costumes or use props! You don't need them. The take should be about your eyes and watching you think and react, not about props and costumes. The only props you should use are a cell phone, your audition pages to indicate papers or a book of some kind, or a purse or bag on your shoulder. If the scene calls for you to be drinking something, you can use water.

Your Slate

Often when you are doing a self-tape or even auditioning in person, you will need to do a "slate." A slate is simply looking directly into the camera lens and saying your name. Depending on the breakdown (again, always read the breakdown!) casting might ask you for your agent, height, location, or even a "hand slate"—where you show the front and back of your hands. Once you've done that, you will do a "full body slate," where you pan up and down so that casting can see you from your feet to the top of your head. If you do not have the ability to pan up and down (you would need someone else working the camera for you), you can edit in a full-body photo of yourself at the end of your slate. Your slate normally will be a separate file from your scenes for the audition—never do a slate and then move right into your scene unless specifically requested by casting. Again, always read the breakdown to see what is required.

Editing and Sending Your Files

There are plenty of actors out there that edit their takes together before sending them in. If you begin your scenes with a good active need to speak and end them with a button before you cut, you should be able to send in the scene as is—without editing it.

If you are editing your files, make sure your need to speak and button have a tiny bit of space in them so you can get a clean edit. And make sure the file isn't too large where you cannot send it. Most agents I've worked with prefer WeTransfer, but there are also Vimeo, YouTube, Dropbox, Google, and so forth.

However: *Read the instructions from casting carefully before shooting your audition or sending in your files!* Some casting offices have very specific ways they want you to shoot the scenes, do the slate, label the files, and send them. Take the time to read the entire breakdown. Read the instructions carefully and follow them or casting won't accept your self-tape.

A Word about Self-Taping for Theater

If your self-tape is for a theater job, the rules of the box will still apply, so you won't alter what you are doing all that much. Depending on the role, I might shoot waist up instead of elbows to top of the head. The people who are casting you for theater roles want essentially the same thing as television and film casting directors:

they want you simply to be the character you are auditioning for and be natural. They want the self-tape to feel like a short film with a beginning, middle, and end. Just because you are auditioning for the theater—even a musical—doesn't mean you need to be much bigger in terms of your acting. Remember that your theater audition is being seen in the box—so the rules of the box still apply.

One thing you must modulate for a theater self-tape is your voice. You can be a bit louder, but remember, the microphone is doing the work, not your trained theater voice. Musical theater auditions—do the same thing. People sometimes feel the need, because it's a musical, to do more gesturing and show, present, or "perform" the song more—not for the camera. Remember the rules of the box. I tell actors who feel they need to do more because it's a musical to look no further than the hit musical *Hamilton*. Watch the actors who are performing solo pieces in that show. Most times they are in a pin spot not doing anything. They are acting the song and allowing the audience to *see* their thoughts; they are making the audience come to *them*. Sounds a bit like what I've been saying in this book. Your self-taped audition for a theater or musical theater role should be no different.

CHAPTER EIGHT

~

After Your Initial Audition
The Callback and Being Put "On Hold"

This is a fun stop along your roadmap to getting on set. After you have either had your on-camera audition in person for a casting director or have sent in your self-tape, you hopefully get "called back." Getting a callback is a good sign! You've done something in your initial audition that the director liked enough to want to call you in again.

When it comes to callbacks for television and film, not much will change from your first audition except perhaps this time, the director will be in the room with you, or virtually on a video conferencing platform. You should try to do everything the same as you did in your initial audition—same choices, same outfit that you originally wore, everything. Remember: they are calling you back because they liked what they saw in your first audition. Stick with what got you there, unless the casting director gives you notes from the director prior to the callback. Check with your agent and make sure there were no adjustments. If you get a note to make an adjustment, do it.

A callback is also called a "director's session." And that's exactly what it is: a session with the director. How your director's session will go completely depends on how the director works. On most of the director's sessions I've been on, I've rarely been directed at all. That doesn't mean you did anything wrong. You will walk into the room and this time the director of the film, television show, or commercial will be there, along with the casting director you auditioned for initially, and maybe a producer or two. Auditioning for commercials will feel different, as directors will tend to work with the actors a bit more. Sometimes the casting director will read the scene with you; sometimes they will watch, along with the director, while you read with an intern or casting assistant. The director will watch your audition on the television monitor. That's right: even though you are in the room with them, usually five feet away, they won't watch you in the room. They will watch you in the box—which is why having a good understanding of the language of on-camera acting is so important.

The only danger of the director's session and having more people in the room is that it may cause you to ramp up your performance. The adrenaline may give you the urge to "perform" or "show."

After all—you have an audience watching you. Resist that urge. Focus on your MAP of beats. Nail them. And most importantly, take your time. Remember, they already like you. Don't push or rush.

If you are lucky to actually receive some direction to try, go for it. If you are unsure of what the director is asking of you, say something. This is your time to get it right, so do your best. Most of the time you won't get complicated direction. They will say something like, "That's great. Tighten it up a bit," which means pick up the pace. Even if you don't completely nail what they are asking you to do, make sure you do at least one thing different from your first take. They want to make sure you can listen and make adjustments on set.

After you hear "Thanks," you are done. Don't expect "Great work!" or "That was awesome." Sometimes it happens, but don't expect it. Just control what you can control and leave it in the room. Actor Bryan Cranston used to take his sides and throw them in the garbage after an initial audition. If he was lucky enough to get a callback, he'd take the sides out of the garbage and start working on them again. Leave your work in the room, because once you leave the room, there is nothing you can do about the outcome. It's out of your hands. Knowing you did your best is all you can hope to feel after a callback.

A Word about Audition Etiquette

I want to say a word about audition etiquette. Like applying for any job—be professional. Always arrive on time. Be respectful and polite. If you go into a casting director's office, be respectful of other actor's preparation in the waiting room. Quietly look over your sides to yourself; don't practice them out loud for the room to hear. If you are reading with another actor and they want to run the scene with you, do so in the hallway or away from the waiting room so as not to disturb others. Stay focused and calm. Don't allow other actors to break your concentration or make you nervous. You have a right to be there as much as anyone.

When you go in to do your audition, read the room. If the director or casting director wants to chat with you, take their lead, but aside from a friendly "Hello," you don't need to engage in conversation with them. You are there to do a job. When you are done and you hear "Thank you," say thanks back and leave the room. Never ask questions like "So when do you think you'll be done casting?" or "Are you going to call my agent to let me know?" Believe it or not, those cringe-worthy moments happen more than they should. Be professional and execute your audition. Do your job and then leave.

Auditioning is such an odd way to apply for a job. The process can be cruel sometimes and there are some nightmare stories out there. Check out the podcast *Dead Eyes* by Connor Ratliff, about an actor getting fired by Tom Hanks from the television show *Band of Brothers*. It's full of audition horror stories, but it will ultimately make you feel better about the process of casting. This is what you've signed up for when you decided you wanted to be an actor. The ride never stops and has many ups and downs, so you just need to be ok with the ride you're on. All you can focus on is your preparation. If you are well prepared, you'll feel good in the room. If you are not prepared, you'll be more nervous. Focus on your MAP, smile to yourself, breathe, and take your time.

Being Put "On Hold," "First Refusal," or "Check Avail"

You nailed your callback. You feel really good about your work. So now if the universe is on your side, you will get the role, right? Well, no. Actually, most times you don't get the part. The SAG-AFTRA numbers of how many of their union members are actually working won't make you want to give up your day job any time soon. You have to be tenacious to be an actor. The more experience you get and the more jobs you book won't make the path any easier. You are a professional job seeker. That's what you've signed up for. So enjoy the ride you're on and keep at it.

Your agent calls you after your callback: you are being put on a first refusal hold. Ok! Is that good? What the hell is that? A first refusal hold is also called a "check avail" or sometimes "icing" or "pinning." You get an audition. You have a callback. If the callback goes well, they will put you on first refusal hold or check avail—which means you are being strongly considered for the role. So much so that they want to put you on hold for the shoot dates. This is a good thing. It means they liked what you did, and you're close to booking it. There is nothing else to be done, but it's not a lock that you'll book it.

Check avail means they are "checking your availability" for the shoot, which may sound redundant. I mean, you had an initial audition where you said you were available, a callback where you said you were available, and now they are checking your availability again? But actors are busy people, and there are many moving parts to production and casting, so this final step before booking is a necessary one.

Now it's a matter of . . . who knows? Maybe they are pairing you up with a family. Maybe the person who they want as your wife isn't available, and they wind up going with a different guy. Maybe the kids they want to cast are already booked on another job. It could be fifty different things. But, if you get put on first refusal hold or check avail, you crushed the audition. Congrats! Celebrate. It's not every day you make it this far. They probably saw three hundred people, called back fifteen to twenty, and it's down to you and perhaps one other person. You are just one step away from hearing those magical words: YOU BOOKED IT!

By the way, it is possible for you to book a job without a callback. I booked *The Chi, Proven Innocent*, and the biggest job of my career, *Contagion*, all without meeting the director or having a callback. Therefore, it's imperative that you learn how to make a good self-tape, because it's the present and the future when it comes to booking jobs, and you may very well book the job without ever being in the room with the director or casting director. It just goes to show you how what you do in the box is everything. Most times, you won't even bring in a picture and résumé when you audition for on-camera jobs. They won't look to see where you went to school or what experience you have. They will cast you based solely on what you do in that box. Practice at home. Learn this language of on-camera and how to speak it well and you will book jobs.

And one more thing—I did not cover "testing" for a role in this book. There are levels when it comes to television roles. I've covered mostly co-star roles in this book, which are generally a day player experience and, most likely, the first job you'll book. It is possible to book these smaller roles (one or two pages of dialogue, maybe one or two days on set) without a callback. *Guest star* roles are meatier, tend to pay more, and your billing in the episode is negotiated. A *recurring* character is one that is in multiple episodes. For a *series regular* role on television (one of the leads of the show), they will sometimes have you "test" for the role. This is a whole separate callback process where you will read with other actors (either previously cast or not) and actually sign your contract before you win the role. You'll most likely build up your résumé with co-star roles and then guest star roles before you audition for a series regular role.

CHAPTER NINE

∼

A Word about Commercials

Like chapter 3, this is a fun but important detour on our roadmap to booking the job and getting on set. Acting in television commercials is an excellent way to make great money while in between television and film jobs or theater work. And as a working actor, you'll need to be able to work in television, film, commercials, and theater to truly make a living. Shoots for television commercials generally last a day or two (truly a day player experience on set), and you can wind up making more money than you would make on an entire twelve-week run of a theater job. But they are a bit like winning the lottery; when the jobs come your way, don't start counting the money before the spot airs. And even when you see your commercial on television, don't count the money. Treat it as "mailbox money": money that "appears" in your mailbox as an unexpected windfall and save it.

Auditioning for commercials is a different experience than auditioning for a television show or a film. There can be a bit more improv to your audition experience, and more so than in films or television shows, they are looking for real people, not actors—moms and dads, grandmas, kids, and so on—real people doing

everyday things. But don't be fooled—nailing a commercial audition can take a great amount of skill.

Usually, commercials are under one minute in length. They air
on television or the internet as fifteen-second, thirty-second, or
one-minute spots, so your objective and role in the spot will be
very clear and to the point. When you audition for a commercial,
you will usually be given a storyboard that shows you, shot by shot,
what the commercial will look like. It could be a woman picking
up a rental car or a guy receiving a delivery from an Ace Hardware
store.

You can use the same technical tricks outlined in chapter 5
to make the copy sound natural: avoid eye locking, use thinking
places, and so on. For commercials, the copy will be minimal, and
lots of times, you won't have any lines at all. Don't forget your
MAP of beats in the script; the same rules apply—map them. On
spots where you have no lines, your beats become everything. You
may have less beats than a television or film script, but you will
definitely have a need to speak and most importantly: remember
your button.

In addition to your trusty MAP technique, here are a few things
to keep in mind when auditioning for commercials versus television and film:

1. *Don't sell anything.* Your job as the actor in the spot is not to
   sell the product. You must have an awareness of the product,
   but you must let the director and the advertising agency sell
   the product. When you try to sell the product, you wind up
   pushing as an actor, and that will prevent you from booking
   the job. You wind up sounding like a salesperson, and that is
   not what you want.
2. *Just be a human.* Most commercials are just people doing
   regular everyday things: laundry, dishes, yard work, and so
   forth. Imagine you are doing these tasks, and there just hap-

pens to be a camera catching you do them. Don't show how you do them for the camera. Just do them. Be simple. The camera will catch everything. It's amazing how many actors do too much when it comes to commercial auditions.

3. *Treat the camera as your friend.* If you are called in to be the spokesperson of the product (like the Sprint guy or the AT&T girl), and you are talking straight to camera, treat the camera as a best friend with whom you are simply sharing a secret. It will remove your desire to sell the product. Did I mention don't sell the product?

4. *And if the spot calls for some comedy . . .* keep reading.

A Word about Comedy

"Dying is easy. Comedy is hard."

—Jack Lemmon

The reason why I chose to address comedy in the commercial section of this book is this: mining the comedy from a television or film comedy script—where you have thirty minutes to two hours to land jokes—is somewhat easier. You simply get more chances to find and land the funny. For a television or film script, being funny isn't the *only* aspect of your skills that you are trying to convey to casting. However, landing a joke in a fifteen- or thirty-second commercial spot? Imperative. And it almost always happens in the button. Watch some commercials today. I guarantee that almost all of them end in a button—and most of them, to comedic effect.

Some of my favorite commercials are the series spots for Progressive Insurance—the "Dr. Rick, Parenta-Life Coach" ads. These spots are full of subtle but comedic acting and *all* end with a button that will make you laugh out loud.

Finding and landing the comedy in a commercial isn't as hard as dying might be, but it's close. I've known and worked with a lot of funny people. It's a skill. There are whole training programs like Second City in Chicago, Groundlings in Los Angeles, and Upright Citizen's Brigade in New York City dedicated to finding the funny. Taking an improv class is always a good idea. It keeps you sharp and teaches you how to think on your feet. Theater auditions rarely have any improv. Television and film auditions sometimes do (and you should always be prepared for a director to throw out an improv scenario for you to try at a callback), but commercials almost always have some form of improv. Whether you are pretending to do yard work or wash the car, or improvising to land a funny bit in a spot, being comfortable with improv and learning how to mine the comedy from a commercial audition is really important if you are going to be successful at them.

Why do a lot of improv actors do well when auditioning for commercials? Because commercial copy is most likely written by someone who is not a television or film writer. It's written by people who are in advertising, and they are writing to sell a product. Many times, the advertisers rely on the actor in the audition room to flesh out their spot and make it funny. And the actor does this for them by improvising. There was a time where ad agencies hired actors to come in and improvise at their offices—and then they would steal the ideas the actors came up with for their advertising campaigns. It's important that the actor understands how to find and land the funny when it comes to auditioning for commercials.

In chapter 1, I told the story of moving to Los Angeles and learning and understanding what my type was. It really helped me find success in the audition room when it came to commercials. It was that understanding coupled with my ability to mine the comedy and find the comedic button for the spots I was called in for that helped me start booking. I once had a callback for a big Mercedes spot directed by a blockbuster film director. We were scientists in a lab testing a Mercedes SUV, and it winds up crashing through a wall unexpectedly. At the end of the take, I slowly looked at the actor playing the boss in the spot as if to say, "Uh-oh." The director loved it and told me to keep it. I didn't get the job, but when I saw the commercial on television, that button was the ending. When it comes to commercials, if it's there, always find the funny in a spot—especially the button.

A Few More Words about Commercials

Let's go back to Chicago. I shot a spot for Ace Hardware—a two-day shoot in July 2018. It never aired, and I never heard anything more about the spot. In July of 2019, I got a text from a friend in L.A. saying, "Just saw your Ace spot. Great job!" After tracking it down and calling my agent, I found out that they decided to air it and just never let us know. It ran for four months, and I made a nice chunk of change. Then one day, it just stopped running, and I was back to being unemployed again. You never know if a spot will run at all or if it does run, how long it will run. It truly is like winning the lottery.

The market for commercials has changed a lot over the years but auditioning for commercials is pretty much the same. The advertising formulas haven't changed much since the 2000s. When you get called in for a commercial, the breakdown will be slightly different and most times, you'll receive an actual storyboard so you can see exactly what happens in the spot and how your role fits in. The scripts for commercials are very fluid. Sometimes after watching the initial round of auditions, they will make changes for the callbacks based on things they felt did or didn't work in the first round of auditions.

In the Ace Hardware commercial, I actually had no lines—which is called an "MOS" spot. There are conflicting theories of the origin of MOS, but one theory is that it stands for "motor only shot" and is a scene where you have no lines. In MOS spots, you will just have an action to perform (such as opening the door and receiving a delivery from an Ace Hardware employee) and when you see the final edit of the spot, there will be music and/or a voice-over playing over your scene.

Here is the breakdown I received for my Ace Hardware callback:

CALLBACK INFORMATION FOR: ACE HARDWARE OC 7/6/18
    Client:
    Stef Tovar
    Status:
    Emailed
    Date:
    Thu, Jul 19, 2018
    Time:
    11:10 AM CDT
    Role:
    Ace Customer
    Warm, friendly, likable, confident. Attractive, yet real, relatable feeling. Smart talented actors. Some roles will have copy and some will just be MOS.
    Wardrobe: Casual
    Rate: See breakdown
    Callbacks:
    07/18/2018, 07/19/2018, 07/20/2018
    Job Dates: 07/23/2018 1st Refusal Hold, 07/24/2018 1st Refusal Hold, 07/25/2018 1st Refusal Hold, 07/26/2018 1st Refusal Hold, 07/27/2018 1st Refusal Hold, 07/28/2018 1st Refusal Hold, 07/29/2018 1st Refusal Hold, 07/30/2018 1st Refusal Hold, 07/31/2018 1st Refusal Hold
    Shoot Dates:
    WEDNESDAY, 7/25 Shoot in store (Norridge);
    THURSDAY, 7/26 Shoot in store (Norridge);
    FRIDAY, 7/27 Shoot in store (Norridge);
    MONDAY, 7/30 Shoot in home (TBD Location);

TUESDAY, 7/31 Shoot in home (TBD Location) (Most likely only needed for one day)
PROJECT INFORMATION
Project:
ACE HARDWARE OC 7/6/18
Type:
Commercial / TV OC
Conflicts:
Home Improvement
Usage:
Intended Use: Broadcast—Class A, Pax/Ion, Cable, Syndication, Internet and Social Media Waiver
Rate:
Scale
Location:
Chicago, IL
Union:
SAG-AFTRA

A couple things of note on a commercial breakdown: conflicts. You cannot audition for similar products. If you have a Lowe's commercial running, you cannot audition for Ace Hardware as that would be a similar product—home improvement. Also, they list all the dates of the shoot and if you were to book the job, you would be on first refusal hold for all the dates—even if you shoot only one day. There's not a lot of flexibility there. If you are put on hold, you have to be available for the shoot—even if they only wind up using you for one day.

I remember when I booked this spot, I was doing a show, *Something in the Game,* a musical about the life of the famous football coach Knute Rockne. I was playing Knute Rockne and was in pretty much every scene of the show. I auditioned for the commercial anyway because again, a good commercial is far more lucrative that an entire run of a show—even if you're playing the lead. Well, I got lucky—not only did I book it, but I shot on a Monday and Tuesday—my two days off from the show. Whew! Again, always check the dates when you read the breakdown. Make sure you are completely available. If you have a day job or are in a show, make sure you can get out of it. You don't want to be the actor who goes in for an audition, says you're available for the shoot, then winds up having a conflict and screwing up the production schedule. This is another reason why there are multiple check avails—actors are busy people and production schedules are always changing. But you never want to be the reason a job gets pushed back. You could lose the job that way.

So, when it comes to commercials, keep it simple. Be real and find the funny if you can. Some of it is a numbers game; some of it is developing a radar to sense when casting for projects is based on appearance versus when the role requires skill and timing. The more auditions you go on, the better chance you have at booking jobs. Keep at it—and nail that button.

CHAPTER TEN

~

What Happens on Set and What to Expect When You Book the Job

You've done it. You have arrived at the final stop on your roadmap. You've finally booked the job! After all the hard work (which included reading and practicing the techniques taught in this book), countless auditions, and first refusals and check avails, you get that call from your agent. You booked it!

What happens next? It may surprise you.

I'm including this chapter in the book for a very important reason: these are things no one tells you—not your agent, not the casting director, not even your college program. It can be nerve-wracking to show up on set for the first time. This will help you know what to expect. Also, once you see what you're in for, you might not get so nervous in the audition room. After booking the job you so desperately coveted, you may think, "Wait. This is it?"

The following information is for when you book co-star work—a role that is one or maybe two scenes of a television show or film, or a commercial. Your experience may be different if you book a lead in a feature film or a series regular or recurring role on a television show. That may include finer treatment, a table read of the script before you start shooting, and as I've touched on, testing for it. But for the purposes of this book, we will look at this chapter as though you were cast in a commercial, as a day player on a feature film, or as a co-star (or possibly guest star) on a television show.

I'm also choosing to focus on co-star work because these roles are sometimes the hardest to execute. There is a great deal of pressure on you to deliver when you are a co-star. Joining a television show like *Law and Order* or *Chicago Med/Fire/PD*, where the cast is established and has been together a long time, and you have to deliver a scene or two with the stars of the show looking to you to not mess up—it's tough. Same with a feature film where you have a scene with an established star—it's hard to not be intimidated and just do your job. This chapter will help prepare you for the moment so you can rise to it.

A Word about Working with Stars

I've had the pleasure of working with quite a few celebrities—Matt Damon, Gwyneth Paltrow, Matt Dillon, Steve Zahn, Fred Willard, Colin Farrell, and some award-winning directors such as Steven Soderbergh and Steve McQueen. Here's the thing: they are there to do a job just like you are. Let them do their job. Take their lead. If they want to talk, be yourself and engage with them, but a lot is asked of them. Don't be that actor that bothers them. Respect their process. Every actor's process is different. Do not ask for selfies with them (at least not before you're done shooting). You'd be amazed how many times I've seen this. Just be professional and do your job.

Once You Are Booked

1. **Keep your phone on. Check your messages.** First, you will most likely get a call from wardrobe. They will want to bring you in for costume fitting. They will want to know as many

of your sizes as you can tell them. Don't lie. Be honest. You will schedule a date and time for your fitting. Wardrobe also may ask you to bring in your own clothes—sometimes as many outfits as you can. Be prepared to pack a suitcase. This is not because they have no budget for costumes. It's because costume designers who work in television and film want you to look natural and wear something you would normally wear, depending on the role. They also may not have time to go shopping for your exact size. Pack a bag with some of your favorite items: jeans, skirt, top, shoes, and belts. Also, pack underwear and socks. Come prepared with what you have in your home. However, if you are playing a doctor, you do not need to bring in scrubs, a lab coat, and the like. They will provide any costume pieces you do not own. This fitting could take place at a studio, on set, or in a completely different location. Also bring ID— your driver's license, social security card, or passport. You'll need it to fill out paperwork. Bring your ID to your fitting and to set when you shoot.

2. **Attend your costume fitting.** Show up on time and with the items they've asked you to bring—to the best of your ability. You may not have any of the items that they are looking for. Just tell them that. Make sure you sign in and keep track of the time you arrive and the time you leave. No one is going to do this for you—not your agent, not wardrobe. This is your business. You are your business. Keep track of these things on your own.

Costume fittings can be fun! Enjoy them. You may meet other cast members there or get information on where you're going to be shooting. I love chatting with wardrobe and hair and makeup. But remember: wardrobe is on a tight schedule and usually under a lot of pressure. Let them do their job.

Be professional. You want to be on time and be in and out. That's the best thing you can do to make their job easier.

3. **Keep your phone on and again: check your messages.** After your costume fitting, the 2nd AD (or second assistant director) will call you prior to the night before your shoot. They will introduce themselves and tell you that you will hear from them soon. Do not bother the 2nd AD if you don't hear from them right away. Be patient. Remember: you are one small piece of this puzzle. It takes a village to make a television show or a movie. Your piece is not more or less important than anyone else's.

You will likely know when your shoot day or days are either from your agent, or if you've booked the job without having an agent, from the casting director, but up until the night before your shoot, you will probably not hear from anyone and even wonder, "Is this job really happening?" That's not unusual. Remember: television and film shoots change daily. They get ahead of schedule. They most definitely get behind. Weather and locations change. Especially on a television show, they really won't know what the daily schedule for your day of shooting looks like until the evening before. Be flexible. Be patient. The 2nd AD will call or text when the schedule for the next day gets approved.

4. **What to do while you are waiting for the call from the 2nd AD:** Prepare! Read the script. Know your scene (or scenes) backward and forward. Analyze it (see chapter 3). Learn who is in the cast (use IMDb.com or the Internet Movie Database app)—especially who your scene partners will be. You most likely will not meet them until you are in the makeup trailer or you walk on set. If you are working on a television show that is currently on air, watch the show! Showing up on set for a television show that is currently on TV without watch-

ing it is like showing up for the first rehearsal of a play not having read it. Do your work. Be prepared.

As a co-star, you need to understand what role you play in terms of the storytelling. You are not hired to carry the show—that's what the stars of the show do. Perhaps you are the villain. Perhaps you are the victim. But generally, co-stars are there to serve the story and be there for the stars of the show. You can still certainly shine in these roles, but it's important to know your place both in terms of the story and professionally.

VERSIONS OF THE SCRIPT: From the time you book the job to the time you walk on set, you will be emailed versions of the full script for the movie or television show. There will be different versions of this script. They will call the versions by color, such as the "PINK script." You may also get individual pages sent to you—a certain scene that changes and is called the "Pink PAGES." You may get one email with one script. You may get ten emails with ten versions of the script. You may have changes to your scene or scenes, you may not. Pay attention to all of the emails. Read the scripts. Look for changes. This is also part of your preparation.

5. **When you finally get the call from the 2nd AD:** It may be 10 p.m. the night before and you need to be on set the next morning at 6 a.m. That happens. Prepare for it. Do as much recon as you can without bothering anyone. If you are really needing to know your call time/location prior to the night before because of childcare or transportation, text the 2nd AD first before calling—in case they are in the middle of shooting. When you do get the call, you'll also receive a "call sheet" (see figures 10.1 and 10.2). On the call sheet you'll have all the info you need: your call time, shooting location, "base camp" location (which is where you will report

CONTAGION

The Keres Corporation
Chicago Production Office

Chicago, IL 60618

DATE: MONDAY DEC. 6, 2010
Hotel LV: 930A

CREW CALL: 1024A

SHOOTING CALL: 11A
Day 45 of 57

Director: Steven Soderbergh
Producer: Michael Shamberg
Producer: Stacey Sher
Producer: Gregory Jacobs
Exec. Producer: Jeff Skoll
Exec. Producer: Michael Polaire
Writer: Scott Z. Burns

Sunrise: 704A   Sunset: 420P
Weather: Mid 20's Mix of Clouds / Sun Shine

SET & DESCRIPTION	SCENE	CAST	D/N	PGS	LOCATION
INT - ER - FAIRVIEW HOSPITAL *Emhoff sits in a isolation room, asks "why them not me"*	35	1, 24, 100, A	D	1 3/8	SHERMAN HOSPITAL 934 Center Drive St. Elgin, Il. 60120
INT - UNIVERSITY ON MINN. HOSPITAL - CLEAN ROOM *Emhoff exits through the lobby, sees man lose it w/ nurse.*	A75	1, 11, 155, 157, A	D	3/8	Crew Parking South West Parking Lot Sherman Hospital 934 Center Drive St.
E/I - UNIVERSITY ON MINN. HOSPITAL *Jory is ushered into Hospital by Doctor & Nurse.*	43	11, 82, 83, A	Dusk 4 N	2/8	Basecamp/ Working Trucks East MRI Parking Lot Sherman Hospital 934 Center Drive St.
INT - UNIVERSITY ON MINN. HOSPITAL - CLEAN ROOM *Emhoff is given a piece of pie.*	44	1, 82, 83, A	N	2/8	
INT - UNIVERSITY ON MINN. HOSPITAL *Jory come to see her father, asks what happen.*	45	1, 11, 46, A	N	1 7/8	Catering Hospital Cafeteria Sherman Hospital 934 Center Drive St.
			TOTAL	4 2/8	

#	CAST AND DAY PLAYERS	ROLE	STATUS	PICK UP	MU/H/WRD	ON SET	REMARKS
1	Matt Damon	Emhoff	W	P/U 845A	945A	1045A	P/U @ Hotel
4	Kate Winslet	Mears	TR	TRAVEL	TRAVEL	TRAVEL	TRAVEL
11	Anna Jacoby-Heron (M)	Jory	W	P/U 1115A	1130A	1230P	P/U @ Hotel / School First
13	Larry Clarke	Swanson	TR	TRAVEL	TRAVEL	TRAVEL	TRAVEL
24	Stef Tovar	ER Doctor	WF	Rpt 930A	930A	1045A	Rpt to Basecamp
46	Gail Rastorfer	Cooler Nurse	SWF	Rpt 3P	3P	4P	Rpt to Basecamp
82	Tom McElroy	University Doctor	SW	Rpt 2P	2P	3P	Rpt to Basecamp
83	Suzanne Lang	University Nurse	SW	Rpt 2P	2P	3P	Rpt to Basecamp
100	Sue Redman	ER Nurse	WF	Rpt 930A	930A	1045A	Rpt to Basecamp
155	TBD	Angry Man	SWF	Rpt 930A	930A	1230P	Rpt to Basecamp/ Fitting First
157	TBD (M)	Anary's Mans Kid	SWF	Rpt 930A	930A	1230P	Rpt to Basecamp/ Fitting First then School

ATMOSPHERE & STANDINS

3 ER Doctors @ 930A Rdy @ 11A
3 ER Nurses @ 930A Rdy @ 11A
4 ND Patients @ 930A Rdy @ 11A
2 ND Patients @ 930A Rdy @ 11A

50 ND Male Adults @ 1030A Rdy @ 12P (8 w/ Cars)
40 ND Females @ 1030A Rdy @ 12P
4 UNI Doctors @ 11A Rdy @ 12P
8 UNI Nurses @ 11A Rdy @ 12P
10 ND Kids (Minors) @ 11A Rdy @ 12P
4 ND Paramedics @ 11A Rdy @ 12P
3 ND Receptionists @ 11A Rdy @ 12P
1 ND Driver for Sc. 43 (Per Transportation)
Total BG: 131

SPECIAL INSTRUCTIONS	
ART DEPT	Sc. 45 - Phone System for Emhoff / Jory, Sc. 45 - Add Window/Sliding Doors Sc. 43 - Dress Ext of Hospital
PROPS	Sc. 35 - Clothes / Cellphone in Plastic Bags, Cup of Pills, Masks & Gloves Sc. 45 - Cooler w/ Blood Sample, Syringes, Vials of Blood, Pumpkin Pie Sc. 43 - Jory's Cellphone, Paperbag w/ Piece of Pie Sc. A75 - Infant Baby Dolls / Strollers
LOCATIONS	Sc. 43 - Police ITC @ Slade & Prospect, Remove Stop Sign, 6 Hair & M/U Stations
M/U & HAIR	Sc. A75 - Some Sick looking Background
VFX	Sc. 43 - Set Extension
COSTUMES	Sc. 45 - Nurses Bio Suit
SPFX	Sc. 35, 43 - Snow & Wetdown, Sc. 45 Sliding Glass Doors
STUNTS	
TRANSPORTATION	Sc. 43 - 1 Minn. D.O.H. Vehicle (W/ Driver)
PRODUCTION	2 Studio Teachers
VIDEO P/B	Sc. 35 - Medical P/B

ADVANCE SHOOTING NOTES

TUESDAY DEC. 7 - DAY 46

INT -EMHOFF'S ROOM / UNIVERSITY HOSPITAL *Mears interviews Emhoff, asks about Beth's travels.*	57	1, 4, 13, A	D	1 6/8	
INT -EMHOFF'S ROOM / UNIVERSITY HOSPITAL *Emhoff watches Mears exit, she leaves pen behind.*	59	1, 4, 13, A	D	1/8	Sherman Hospital 934 Center Drive St. Elgin, Il. 60120
INT -EMHOFF'S ROOM / UNIVERSITY HOSPITAL *Emhoff asks Mears if Jory is safe, she can't get it, right.*	AA75	1, 4, 13, A	D	6/8	
INT -D.O.H. VEHICLE *Jory is being Driven to see her father.*	42	11, A	N	2/8	EPK ON SET

WEDNESDAY DEC. 8 - DAY 47

INT - WILLOWBROOK MALL *Emhoff tell security guard, it'll be back to normal soon. *** company move ****	159	1, 127, A	D	6/8	North River Mall 7501 W. Cermak Rd. Chicago, IL 60546
INT - FUNERAL HOME - MINNESOTA *Manger tells Emhoff that he can't take the bodies.*	E84	1, 127	D	5/8	*** company move ***
INT - FUNERAL CHAPEL - MINNESOTA *Emhoff and Beth's Mother discuss options*	F84	1, 27	D	1 0/8	WMH Scott Funeral Home 1100 Greenleaf Ave Wilmette, IL 60091

THURSDAY DEC. 9 - DAY 48

EXT - STREETS - MINNESOTA *Emhoff & Jory see burning building, Tells her to put on her mask*	A123	1, 11, X, A	D	4/8	
INT - MARKET - MINNESOTA *Emhoff see everyone looting. Jory takes box of oatmeal.*	B123	1, 11, X, A	D	1 1/8	TBD EPK ON SET

FRIDAY DEC. 10 - DAY 49

EXT - BRYANT PARK - MINNESOTA	B142	1, 124, 135, 136, X, A	D	1 1/8	1408 Covington // Lincoln St & Chance Av.

Figure 10.1. Here is my callsheet from *Contagion*. Notice my number: 24. Each actor has a number and under "Cast" you'll see the order of scenes they are shooting that day and which ones you are in according to your cast number.

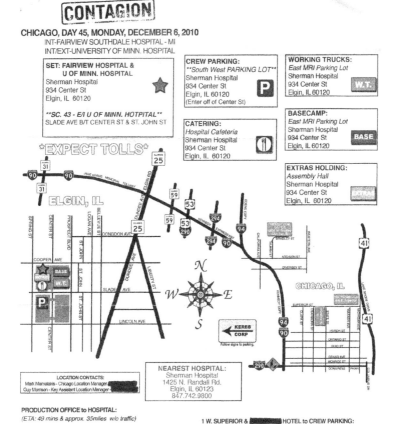

Figure 10.2. On page two of the callsheet is a map with directions, addresses and phone numbers.

to first), your fellow cast members, and the entire production team's names and titles. It will also most likely include a map of where to park, as shown in figure 10.2, and other helpful information. Nowadays with a variety of GPS apps for your phone, you can simply punch in the address of your base camp and find your way easily. The call sheet will also have the scenes they plan to shoot that day. You'll see your scene or scenes on there, and based on your call time, you'll have some sense of how long of a day you can expect. Now that can change instantly, so don't bet on it, but at least you'll have some idea of how your day will go.

You should also try to learn a few names off the call sheet, and not just the director. Most times, the director and the writer will not be with you on set as you shoot your scene. They are at monitors in a separate area (sometimes known as "Video Village") watching along with producers. You will want to know the names of the folks who will be on set with you as you are shooting your scene: ADs (there are two—1st and 2nd ADs), DP (director of photography), boom op, and especially the camera operators. The camera operators will be able to tell you placement, frame size, movement of the shot, and so forth.

When You Show Up on Set

1. **Be on time.** I cannot stress it enough, and I shouldn't even have to put it in this book, but here it is: be on time. Seriously. Do not start your day on set by getting there late. Period.
2. **Report to base camp.** Once you park you will be directed to base camp. Base camp most likely will include the production "office" (usually a trailer), the hair and makeup trailer, wardrobe trailer, actor trailers, and your trailer. Yes, you finally get to say, "I'll be in my trailer." But just be prepared.

Sometimes you get lucky when it comes to a trailer, but most of the time you'll be in a honeywagon: one large trailer with several private "rooms." Your room will have your character's name taped on the door—something fancy like "Doctor #1" or "White Donor." (These are a couple of my personal favorites from my career.) Your luxurious room may consist of a small sink, a mirror (sometimes), a cushioned bench to sit down on, a toilet that may or may not work, and your costume. And most importantly, if you are a member of SAG-AFTRA (and even if you're not) your paperwork for the job, which includes your contract.

3. **Look over your paperwork carefully.** Make sure the day rate and your agent's (or your) info is correct. This is how you will be paid; make sure it is correct. Again: this is *your* job; this is *your* business—not your agent's and not anyone's that is working on set that day. It is your job alone. Take pictures of your paperwork with your phone just in case. That way if you sign it in a hurry and your agent asks later, you can show them what you signed. If you have questions before you sign it—WAIT to sign it. Talk to your agent. The paperwork should be laid out with tabs at the places you need to sign or initial. If you have questions, ask. Do not be afraid to ask. Also, there will be a mini version of the call sheet along with the script pages for the day. Make sure to take the time to look it over, and make sure there were no changes made to the script between the time you saw the latest version (whichever color that turns out to be) and the day of shooting. Keep those pages with you. You will see other actors, including the stars of the show, looking at them.

4. **Get into hair/makeup and costume.** Most likely, you will be brought into hair and makeup prior to your putting on your costume. I love the hair and makeup trailer. Here you will meet the folks who have been working on the television show or film every day. They are in the trenches. They've

got stories. And if you are late or wind up being a problem of any kind, the director will hear about it from them. You may also meet fellow actors, including the stars of the show. If it's your first time on set, you'll be nervous and excited. Be professional. Be yourself. Treat it as a job, and let people come to you. You are walking into a family—a group of people who most likely have worked together before. Your job is to get in and out of hair and makeup, so they can move on to the next actor. You don't want to be the cause of any delay for the hair and makeup folks.

5. **Back to your trailer to . . . hurry up and wait.** The 2nd AD or whoever will be ushering you back and forth between hair and makeup, your trailer (or holding area), and set will give you some idea of how long you'll have to wait before you're due on set. Get into your costume and prepare. Then . . . wait. The stories you hear about waiting all day to shoot something are true. Long waits happen. However, it's your job to be ready to go whenever they knock on your door. It doesn't matter how long they've made you wait. It doesn't matter if you've waited six hours and you're tired, hungry, and so on. When it's time to shoot your scene, you need to be ready to go. Everyone fills this time differently, and I'm not here to instruct you how to fill it. The 2nd AD may tell you, "Grab some food or hit crafty." Crafty is also known as "craft services" and it's where you find snacks, water, beverages, and small bites. Depending on the set, you may also be able to grab breakfast, lunch, or dinner. And if you work for more than six hours on a SAG-AFTRA set, they have to feed you a meal. Enjoy the free food! If you have dietary restrictions or have a set way that you eat your meals throughout the day, bring your own snacks rather than relying on crafty. You never know what will be there, and some sets are better than others. However, I am generally blown away by crafty and what they serve for meals on set. The food

is almost always amazing and one of the highlights of working in television and film. Until it's time to shoot your scene, read a book or watch something on your iPad or phone, but stay sharp and focused. You don't want to get the call to set and not be ready to go. I recommend going over your scene or scenes and staying prepared. You'll see why below.

It's Time: What to Expect
When You Walk on Set to Shoot Your Scene

The first time you get called to set is for a rehearsal. That's right! You actually get to rehearse! Don't get too excited though. This rehearsal isn't really for you. It's to set up the shot. This is where the director, 1st AD, and the DP decide what the shot will look like. If there's movement like walking down a hallway while the actors in the scene are talking, they'll decide how the scene will move as well, and most importantly, how they will light it.

You, of course, are a part of that decision making, but so are the other actors and the art direction—anything else that will be in the shot. You are essentially a prop—and they will sometimes treat you like one. Don't take it personally. You just focus on your job, which seemingly will sound very easy, but it is more complicated than you think.

Depending on the size of the role you have if you are a co-star (and definitely if you are a guest star), you will have a "stand-in." Someone whose job is to physically stand in for you while they focus lights and set up the shot. When you get called to set, you may hear "first team to set." The "first team" consists of the actual actors who they will be shooting when they roll the camera. The second team will be the stand-ins who they use to set up the shot.

You'll be fitted with a microphone when you arrive on set. It may happen before or after rehearsal. They will hide the mic, so it will either go on your waist, on your ankle, or perhaps on your back. It's tricky how they hide it, but just listen to the sound department and trust them. They've done it a thousand times. Make sure wherever you decide to put the mic, you're able to execute the business of the scene with it and work with the sound engineer to make sure it's comfortable.

Once you Arrive on Set for Rehearsal

1. **Be on time and well prepared.** This may sound like a given, and I know I've covered this, but I'm putting it first on this list for a reason. It's the number one mistake I see inexperienced actors make, and it could be detrimental to your career. It shows a lack of respect for the director, crew, and stars of the show. Be on time and ready to deliver your scene or scenes.

2. **Listen.** Take in what the director and others are telling you. Get names and remember them. The director, 1st AD, and others will usually ask you your name, but don't be offended if they don't. They are moving very fast and every second costs money. It's not a place to get personal. You're there to do your job. If the stars of the show goof around or make jokes, they've earned the right to do so. Your job is to be professional (and to be yourself, of course).

3. **Learn where your "mark" will be.** Once you block the scene with the director and other actors, you will be given a mark on set—usually a piece of tape on the floor—which is where you are to stand when they call "Action!" That's your starting place. Take note of it. Most often, there will be someone whose job it is to follow the actors around, ninja-like, and place tape on the floor for the actor's marks. Each actor will be a different color of tape. It is usually a "T" shaped mark and it's important that your feet fit "into" the T and not over it or behind it. If you stand incorrectly on your mark, you could be blocking another actor or yourself. The T determines body/face direction for the DP, which

helps lighting and camera. You want to be able to feel where your mark is with body awareness, muscle memory, or on-set visual cues. Make sure you remember where your mark is.

4. **Make sure you can repeat any movement.** As you run through the scene (usually the director will lead the rehearsal, but sometimes the 1st AD will lead or even the DP), take note of your movement. If you have business (such as typing or office work if you are sitting at a desk or literally anything other than just standing in one place the whole time) take note of that as well. You'll need to repeat your movements the exact same way for every take.

5. **If the script calls for you to use a prop, ask about it.** If your character uses a prop in the script, you may want to ask about it now. You may not get to use it prior to shooting, but if it's really important to you and your action in the scene, ask about it—jewelry as well (a wedding ring, watch, etc.).

6. **Run the lines and beats.** If you can, and most often you won't be able to, try using your MAP technique in rehearsal—make sure any beats in the scene you want to take are repeatable and try them. Your beats should not be radically different from your audition or your callback. Don't walk on set for rehearsal after getting cast from a taped audition or in-person callback and do something completely different. You won the role with what you brought to the audition and callback. That's what they are expecting to see. There of course will be some variation, and you may even get some new direction, but stick with what got you there. At least for your first run-through at rehearsal.

One Last Word on Rehearsal

Every rehearsal and every director are different. You never know what you're going to get. All you can do is be prepared. There are a hundred variables; be ready for anything. Some actors like to bring it in rehearsal, some use the rehearsal as a general sketch of the scene and save it for performance. Feel the room and make sure you use your rehearsal to be as prepared as possible to shoot the scene.

After Your One Rehearsal

After your one rehearsal, you get to—guess what? Wait! Again! That's right. Your glamorous day on set continues and they bring back the second team and you get to relax while they set the shot, focus the lights, and prepare the camera. You may get to go back to your trailer. They may keep you in a holding area. The holding area may have director-style chairs that say "Cast" on them for you to sit in. They may not. Regardless, I wouldn't wander too far. Here's the moment where you really need to be ready to go. Do what you need to do to prepare and stay out of everyone's way. Every actor is different. If you need a space that's more private to go over your scene, know that it just might not be available to you. Unlike the theater, where you can find a corner, maybe have some privacy, and run through a scene or monologue, you are sharing a set with sometimes a hundred other people—crew, actors, extras. You will truly feel like a small piece of the puzzle.

Just remember: You are no less important to the final product than anyone else in the room. You are also no *more* important, and in fact, you will most likely feel like a prop. That's part of the job. If your co-stars or the stars of the show want to run lines with you, do it. Most likely they won't, but if you have any chance of running the scene with them again, take it.

Before "Action!"

It's time. The first team is called back, and they are ready to shoot. You are brought back to set. You relieve your stand-in, and you are ready to go. Here are some things to consider:

1. **The set may look different from rehearsal.** You should expect that. They've had time to dress it. There may be lights where you haven't seen them, for example; but you still need to hit your mark and do exactly what you did in rehearsal unless you are told otherwise.

2. **Your mark may be gone.** The giant piece of tape that was there for you in rehearsal may not be there. There may only be a small dot of tape (usually the same color as your old mark) there for you to hit your mark. Don't let it throw you. That's why it's important to learn how to hit your mark by feeling it. This is easier said than done and requires some reps to get used to doing it. But in rehearsal, don't rely solely on your floor mark. Use the furniture. Use your fellow actors. Get a feel of where production needs you to be when you are on your correct mark.

3. **You may be given a prop.** After your one rehearsal, it may have been decided that your character is holding a glass of wine or a clipboard. It may be handed to you right before you shoot your scene. If you asked about a prop, this is when you will get it. Get familiar with it as fast as you can. You may only get a couple of minutes with it. Do the best you can. Make sure whatever action you do with the prop is repeatable.

4. **Extras.** If the scene calls for "background" or "extras," they will also be on set with you now. There will be someone in charge of them that will instruct them and move them like props. You may be shooting a party scene and get friendly with an actor, only to have them switched out for another actor wearing a different color. It's all about how the shot looks in the lens for the director. They will tinker with it up until the last minute and beyond. Be prepared for that. Extras are important to the scene, and you need to look like you are interacting naturally with them. But stay on target: your focus in the scene is what you worked on and did in your audition and rehearsal.

"Action!"

It's the moment you've been waiting for—the end of your journey! Finally. It may have been hours since you sat in the makeup trailer (and hair and makeup will now be on set to do touch-ups for you and the cast), but here you are. This is the moment for you to do your job, to serve the scene and forget about everything else. Easy, right? There's only a crew of fifty, thirty-five extras, countless others just visiting the set to watch, and of course, your fellow scene partners. Actors, who could be the star of the show, looking to you to deliver your lines and give them what they need to execute the scene. So, don't mess up.

Seriously though, whenever someone says that acting is easy, that anyone could do it—especially on-camera acting—remind them of the pressure of this moment and ask them if they really could do it. But there is a reason you are there—remember that. This is what you've trained for. This is why you bought this book. You've nailed the audition and booked the job, prepared, been professional, on time, and ready to go. So . . . breathe. Trust that your preparation will be there and just be present, and before they say, "Action!," smile (to yourself). You've got this.

What to Expect While You Are Shooting Your Scene

Again, every set is different, and you should be prepared for any number of things to happen. Just keep listening and executing. Here are some things you should be prepared for:

1. **Be prepared to get no direction.** Once you begin shooting your scene, you may not get a single piece of direction for anything you are doing. Don't let that throw you. Remember: the director, 1st AD, DP, and yes, the producers are looking at a hundred different things—only one of which is

your performance. On a commercial shoot, you may get more interaction from the director than on a television or film shoot, but you never know. If no one is giving you direction, that could very well mean that you are doing a great job. Just keep on that path until you hear differently. If they move on to the next take, that means they are happy with what they got. Honestly, no news is good news.

2. **Know how to find your lens and light.** When you are getting ready to actually shoot the scene, have a sense of which camera (or cameras) are on you. Find your lens. Make sure you are not blocked from view. This is where knowing the names of the camera operators comes in handy. You can always ask them which camera is on you, how tight the shot is, and so on. If you can't see the camera, the director can't see your performance. It's the same with lighting. Is there a key light or other specific lighting on you that you should stay in? Learn how to feel the light on your face.

3. **There will be different angles and takes for the same scene.** Depending on the scene, the story, and the like—you may be doing "coverage" for the scene or multiple "POVs" (points of view), and you need to be prepared for that. For example, depending on the scene, you will most likely shoot a wide shot or a "master shot" as well as POVs. The "master" is where we see all actors and action from a wider angle. Then they will "push in" and do closeups, or a shot from one or all the actors' POVs. Here's where you'll need to do exactly what you did in the master shot, just closeup. Having an awareness of the size of the shot will help you make adjustments to your volume, physicality, and so on. In your medium closeup, you may have to hold that prop just a little higher depending on the needs of the DP.

Sometimes when they shoot the master (depending on the budget), they will have multiple cameras shooting closeups at the same time. If you are doing a closeup where the camera is over your shoulder and you are not in the shot, you still need to give the same performance you gave your fellow scene partners in the master. This time, keep your movement smaller and more contained without blocking their coverage. Your co-stars and stars of the show are depending on you to give them the goods so they can do their job and deliver their closeup. They will, in turn, do the same for you if you have a closeup.

Be mindful of overlapping dialogue—unless it's specifically in the script and you rehearsed the scene that way. It can be tricky for editing and you always want to make sure the stars of the show can be heard clearly. Same with closing a door on someone's line, setting down a prop, and so forth.

4. **Don't assume you will get multiple takes.** Some directors like to do multiple takes of a scene. Some like knocking it out in one or two takes. Don't save your favorite choice for later. You may not get to do it. And once the master shot has been done, you'll need to repeat exactly what you did in the closeups—deliver the goods as best you can on the first take.

5. **Expect things to change.** The crew may discover as they begin to shoot that something needs to change. It could be a lighting issue, or it could be dialogue. Don't take this as a reflection of your work. Just keep focused and executing the scene. It may feel really technical—that's because it is. There is precision in hitting your mark and saying your lines the exact same way multiple times. It's just part of the job. If you get changes thrown at you, just go with them.

6. **When you get direction, listen to it, and take it.** If you don't understand what the director is asking you to do, stop and ask. Make sure that what you do in the new take is different from what you did in the previous take. There will be a lot of pressure for you to move quickly and execute, but if

you need a second to process or try it first, ask for it and take it. It's better to do that than to have everyone reset and roll camera, only for you to not do what is being asked of you and have to cut and start over.

This is important: don't let it throw you if the director asks during your take, while the camera is still rolling, to go back and pick up a scene in the middle. This is another way that theater is different from television and film. You may be interrupted and given direction in the middle of a take—asking you to repeat a moment or pick up the scene from a particular line. Being able to jump to any part of the scene without the director having to explain why is an excellent on-camera skill to have.

What to Expect after You've Shot Your First Scene

Again, be present and prepared. It could be a long day, or you may be doing just one or two shots. You need stamina to work in television and film because you have to be prepared to shoot at a moment's notice. You have to be able to deliver the same performance you gave in the master for any other coverage—even if it shoots hours after or sometimes even the day after. There are people on sets that are hired to maintain "continuity," making sure every little detail is checked. Was your top button buttoned in the scene when you shot it yesterday? Continuity will make sure, but it's your job too. Take note of these details. It will only make you more valuable and more likely to be hired back.

Once you have shot your last scene and all your coverage has been done, you will be "wrapped." This means that the job (for you) is over. Sometimes they will make a thing of it and announce, "That's a wrap for Stef!" and you may get a round of applause. But usually? You are told they no longer need you. You take off your mic, and you slip away to your trailer to get out of costume while the crew prepares for their next shot. You may have never even been told if you did good work or be given a thank you. Again, don't take it personally. It's a job, it's finished, and you are moving on to your next one.

Before You Leave

After you have gone back to your trailer to change, but before you leave, do the following:

1. **Make sure you have everything.** If you used some of your own clothes for a costume piece and you are officially wrapped for the shoot, take that piece with you. Double check that you didn't leave anything behind in your trailer.
2. **Hang up your costume.** It may be a little thing but leave your costume the way you found it. Don't be that actor that throws their costume on the floor.
3. **Sign out.** Make sure you sign out! Make a note of when you signed in and out—and if you took a meal break. It's your job to log those things for yourself so that when you are paid, everything matches up. If there's a discrepancy when you are paid, your agent can't help you if you didn't keep a good record. You can even use your phone and take a picture of your sign out sheet.

And that's it! Your glamorous day on set is done and you are back at it the next day looking for your next job. You hope that the work you did was good and that you don't end up on the cutting room floor. But remember: what you did is something many dream of doing and never get the chance to do. Don't take it for granted. Every day that you get the opportunity to work as an actor in this business is a day to be celebrated. Enjoy the ride.

CHAPTER ELEVEN

~

When Luck Meets Preparation

I teased a bit of this story in the first chapter, but . . . how does one get to do a scene opposite Matt Damon (and Gwyneth Paltrow)? Well, read on and you will be amazed as to how it all played out.

In August of 2010, I was living in Chicago and got a call from my agent to audition for a film. It was one line—a guy at a dinner party. The character's name was "Dan." My line was "It's Tur-ducken. It's turkey, chicken, and duck." I went on tape for it and forgot about it. A couple of months later, I got another call from my agent, "Congrats! You booked the Steven Soderbergh movie!"

"What Steven Soderbergh movie?" I asked.

"The one you auditioned for a while back," he said.

I said, "I didn't audition for a Steven Soderbergh movie."

He said, "Yes, you did. It's called *Contagion*."

Well, ok! He said he would call back with the details.

The next day he called me back and said, "Great news. They are bumping you up. Instead of the role of Dan, you're going to be ER Doctor." I said, "Well that sounds like a demotion. I was play-ing a character with a name and now I'm just some doctor?" He said, "Trust me it's a bigger role. The script is top secret, but when I get it, I'll pass it on to you." I got the script a couple days later and read it. It was incredible. The role of the ER Doctor was at the beginning of the movie in a critical scene that was 6 pages long. Then I went on IMDb.com. I found out that my big scene would be with Matt Damon.

My first thought was, *this has to be a mistake.* I technically didn't even audition for this. How was I being trusted with this crucial role in the movie (which was loaded with movie stars) when I had not even auditioned for it or met the director? I thought at any moment I would get another call from my agent telling me "Hey, sorry. They are actually bringing in a star to play the doctor." I seriously thought I would never actually shoot the movie. I even emailed the pro-duction coordinator after he sent me an updated script and asked, "Should I prepare all three scenes?" He immediately forwarded my email to the folks at Carmen Cuba Casting, who were very sweet, and said, "Yep! You are to prepare all three scenes!"

I had a little over a month to prepare for the shoot, so I went to work. When I auditioned, I was clean shaven with no glasses that day. I thought, if I'm going to be in a closeup with Matt Damon,

I want to look as different from him as possible, so I grew a beard. The scene took place in an ER, so I called a friend from college, Amy Smith, who was then head nurse in a level-1 trauma unit at a hospital in Long Island, New York. She had seen just about everything there was to see coming in and out of that ER. I read the scene to Amy over the phone, and she was immensely helpful. There was a lot of technical, medical jargon for me to say:

ER DOC

We don't always know. Some people get a disease and live. Some become sicker and die. My best guess is that it was either meningitis or encephalitis and with encephalitis we're in the dark 90 percent of the time—if it was summer I might say a bug bite.

West Nile. Herpes can cause encephalitis. Any number of things can. We can tell you how, but not always why. Her blood work indicated some sort of massive infection—that's how.

With Amy's help, I looked up and learned what every single word meant so that when I walked on set, I would feel totally prepared. Working with Matt Damon, Gwyneth Paltrow, and Steven Soderbergh was going to be nerve wracking. Remember, the only way to calm your nerves is preparation. The more prepared you are, the less you will feel like you don't belong there. I knew walking on that set with the likes of those folks, I would already feel like I didn't belong there. I made sure I put in the work.

I went to my costume fitting with a full beard and glasses—completely different from my audition tape (and something I've said *not* do in this book). I didn't meet Steven or anyone in the cast. Wardrobe took a photo of me in my doctor's outfit and I was done.

A few days later, on a chilly December day in 2010, I went to set. It was an abandoned hospital in the northwest suburbs of

Chicago, close to where I went to high school. Call time was 7:30 a.m. I arrived at seven. I was the first one there, even ahead of the 1st AD. I remember thinking the whole night before, "I'm going to get a call from my agent telling me they made a mistake, and I'm not shooting this movie." I check in with security on set:

Me: I'm just checking in. I'm one of the actors.

Security: Which role?

Me: ER Doctor.

Security: Which ER Doctor?

Great, I thought; I knew it. Someone else is playing the ER doctor, and I'm going to be some kind of background doctor. I checked in and made my way to the holding area. The first scene I was shooting was the one where Gwyneth Paltrow is in the ER with Matt Damon. She's in bed and has a seizure, and I rush in to take care of her. There's nothing in the script that tells me what I'm physically doing to help her. My lines are just some standard medical questions that I ask Matt while I'm working on her, so the scene is really just about the action, but we hadn't discussed what that action would be.

Steven says, "Here we go with rehearsal. Action!" We begin to run the scene with the lines. I stop.

Me: Can I ask a question really quick?

Steven Soderbergh: Sure.

Me: What am I doing here physically?

On-Set Doctor: Well, she's having a seizure so she's experiencing—

Me: Yep. I understand her symptoms, but what am I physically doing to help this woman?

Steven Soderbergh (to On-Set Doctor): Yeah. What is Stef physically doing to help her?

Bam! In that moment, I took a breath, asked for what I needed, and showed an Oscar-winning director that I came prepared. We devised a plan for the physical action of the scene. I asked Oscar-winner Gwyneth Paltrow if I could put my hand on her face, and we shot the first take. We reset and did it again, this time with Gwyneth moving her head in the opposite direction. "We got it. Moving on." Steven said. We did it in just *two takes*.

In that second take, Oscar-winner Matt Damon improvised a bit. He broke up the lines, added a couple of words (see chapter 5), and made it all sound natural because he's a damn pro. So I decided I would try the same. Although I had more medical jargon to say that didn't allow for me to add much, on my entrance right after "Action!," I looked right at Matt and asked, "What's your wife's name? Is it Beth?" He totally went with it and replied, "Um, yeah—It's Beth." We shot the scene. Nailed it.

Bam again! In that moment, I showed the star of the movie that I was prepared and came to play. I didn't add the line to one up him, just to rise to his level. I knew my place and my role in the film, and I was there to serve the stars and the story. I was there to work. In that little moment in the ER, I showed the director, writer, and stars that I could do it. Thank God, because I was still worried I was going to be replaced at any moment. The big scene where I come out into the lobby and tell Matt that Gwyneth had died wasn't going to be filmed until the afternoon, so I had time to take a look at it again, calm my nerves, and reset. That is until the 1st AD came over and said, "So we're going to shoot Gwyneth's other scene in the afternoon and move right to the lobby scene. You ready?" Gulp—I guess so. Here we go.

The crew was setting up, and we did a rough rehearsal of the action of the scene as written. Then we shot one and something wasn't right. On a break, I saw Matt, Steven, and the brilliant screenwriter, Scott Burns, sitting down and discussing the scene, and I wandered over to eavesdrop on their conversation.

As written, the scene in the lobby began *after* Matt's character had already received the news of Gwyneth's death:

Mitchell Emoff and his son Clark watch a MINNESOTA WILD game on TV.

MITCHELL'S POV

The ER DOCTOR and a SOCIAL WORKER IN A BUSINESS SUIT come down the hallway. Mitchell sees them and gets up.

EMHOFF

You let me know what happens on the power play, Clarky. I'm gonna go talk to the doctor.

We don't have to hear every word to know what's being said, just fragments of conversation punctuated by grim body language. The force of the news collapses Emhoff. The Social Worker's voice is soothing.

SOCIAL WORKER

I know this is hard to accept.

EMHOFF

I just . . . I don't understand.

ER DOC

We have people here who can help with the arrangements.

SOCIAL WORKER

Maybe the boy has a friend he can stay with while you begin to deal with this. I understand he's your stepson.

Mitchell nods.

EMHOFF

He has a friend down the street. His biological father lives in Duluth.

SOCIAL WORKER

I'll go speak with him.

The SOCIAL WORKER walks toward CLARK. Mitchell turns to the ER DOC.

From what I could gather when eavesdropping, having the scene pick up after he received the news didn't feel right to Matt. We had also lost a some of dialogue from the scene we just shot in the ER where Gwyneth was having her seizure.

As written, the scene played very much like a husband receiving the sad news of the passing of his wife, but Matt wanted something more. He wanted to focus on the shock of his character, and Scott and Steven were trying to figure out how to help him with it. I very casually, and without pushing, offered to rearrange my dialogue to include some of what was cut in the previous scene—to help Matt get where he needed to go emotionally, since I was the one doing most of the talking while Matt reacted. I also offered to add some new dialogue they were writing, including the "Mr. Emhoff, I'm sorry: your wife is dead" line. I remember Scott looking at me with disbelief and saying, "Can you do that?" I said, "Sure. No problem." If you watch the scene in the film, you'll find it very different from what was originally conceived on the page.

I had worked on the scene so many times on my own, I was so prepared, that moving the dialogue around, and even improvising a bit, wasn't a problem. We shot the scene and it turned out to be a pivotal moment in the movie. Matt Damon, when interviewed on various talk shows, frequently would say it was his favorite scene of the film (and he was exceptional in the scene). At the wrap party, Steven came up to me and said, "You know, your scene with Matt was a critical moment of the movie. I knew it. Matt knew it. If you tanked that scene, we were in big trouble. You kicked ass. Thank you for your work." That night at the wrap party, Matt and I hung out like we were old college friends and had a great time.

Postscript: I shot *Contagion* in December of 2010. In April 2011, I was in my apartment and getting ready to head out for the day. My beard had been getting itchy, and I decided it was time to shave for spring. I was in my bathroom lathered up with shaving cream when I got a phone call on my cell. It was a number I didn't recognize, but I decided to pick it up:

Woman: Hi, is this Stef?

Me: Yes, it is.

Woman: Hi, this is ____. I'm calling from Steven Soderbergh's office.

Me: . . .

Woman: Hello?

Me: Um. YES. Hi!

Woman: Well, I'm calling because Steven really loved your work on the film, and they've written a new scene they would like to shoot with you and Matt in May. So, we were wondering if you were in town and available, and if you still have that great beard you had in December.

Me (staring in the mirror with shaving cream on my face): (Beat). Um, yes. Yes, I've still got it. I'm in town and would love to shoot another scene.

Woman: Great. When we know more details, we'll reach out to your agent. Thanks!

It turned out that Matt had shaved his head for his next project, and we never got to film the new scene, but still, that was a fun phone call to get—a nice affirmation that the work I did on the film was well received. There was another scene we did shoot in December that didn't make it into the film. In that scene, Matt was put into quarantine, and I was asking him questions wearing hazmat gear. It was a fun one, and I was bummed it didn't make it into the film. We laughed a lot, and he was a lot of fun to work with. It was a once in a lifetime shoot and experience.

Once the movie came out, my scene was in every trailer for the film. I had people calling, texting, and emailing me. For the SAG Awards that year, they had a segment called "What SAG actors are doing all over the country—not just in Hollywood." They showed my scene and had my name up on the screen alongside it. This was at the SAG Awards—with all those famous actors watching, broadcast all over the world. I sent Steven a letter thanking him. He wrote a very nice note back, which I have framed in my office. I've continued to work in television and film since, but this was truly my fifteen minutes of fame.

I tell this story not to boast of my accomplishment but to illustrate to aspiring actors hoping to break into television and film that it was pure luck that I landed the biggest job of my career (so far)—absolute luck. I didn't even audition for it—but when the moment came for me to deliver, I was prepared and rose to that moment.

You now have a roadmap that takes you step by step from getting an on-camera audition to what is expected of you on set—along with a solid understanding of the language of on-camera acting, something I didn't have early in my career and wished that I did. I relied on a lot of trial and error—and luck. Luck will certainly be a factor in your career, but now you'll be well prepared for when that moment comes along.

When I got the job on *Contagion*, I made the most of it. I prepared so much that when the time came to deliver, I didn't think twice. I didn't have time for nerves. I just did the work because it's a job. On-camera work feels like a job because, unlike theater, it's a very technical craft. You finish the job and move on to the next—and hopefully find ways to enjoy the ride.

The moral of this story? Preparation and luck: you need this combination to work. On-camera work is a job, and you are always on the lookout for your next one. The road an actor travels is exhausting, frustrating, scary, and unstable. But it's rewarding. And if you work hard and really master this new language of on-camera acting, you'll start booking jobs. You may even land *your* fifteen minutes of fame.

Acknowledgments

I first and foremost want to thank Damon Kiely, a friend and mentor who helped me become a better teacher, encouraged me to write this book, and who was instrumental in lighting the spark that made it better; Lauren Sheely (my editor before I submitted my first draft), for making this book so much better than I could have on my own; John Cerullo, Barbara Claire, Ashleigh Cooke and everyone at Applause Books for their support; Andrea Bendewald, for her friendship and for helping to recall our story and make it even funnier; Brandy O'Briant, for a first edit and advice—(her Page1 Books is an amazing book delivery service); Matthew Miller, for believing in me enough as an on-camera coach to send actors my way and for giving me notes on the book that were absolute game changers; Marco Fargnoli, for telling me what directors on set *really* want actors to be able to do; Brandon Dahlquist, for his friendship and his awesome photography (www.brandondahlquist-photography.com); my pictured actors (and students!): Rochelle Therrien and Terry Bell; Johnny Clark, for his belief in me as an actor and writer; Carrie Johnson, my former agent who stuck with me during those two years when I wasn't booking anything in L.A.; Todd Turina and everyone at Stewart Talent Chicago, who navigated my *Contagion* experience; Lisa Roth and Cassie Slater, for their help, encouragement, and love; Haley Carlson, for her subtle mindset coaching and the belief she instilled me; Susan Haimes, for being the mother I needed during this process; Katie-Sarah Phillips, for being my home base; Karen Camelet, for being an amazing mom to Sam and being proud of me; my teachers: Bruce Cromer, my college professor and mentor at Wright State University, for his guidance, and Don Haefliger, who sent me down the path of being an actor when I was just in high school; Emily Rohm, who first encouraged me to coach actors years ago—who watched me fail and helped me get better at it—thank you. To ALL my students I've coached over the years—thank you for allowing me to be your teacher and helping to shape the MAP technique. And to Sam, for growing up backstage with me, letting me use his room to tape actors, and never blinking an eye at the crazy path his dad chose in life. I love you.

~

Resources

Recommended Books

On the Craft of Acting

A Practical Handbook for the Actor, by Melissa Bruder, Lee Michael Cohen, Madeleine Olnek, Nathaniel Pollack, Robert Previto, and Scott Ziegler (New York: Random House, 1986). This book takes Stanislavski's "Method" and distills it into a practical guide that is easy to apply to scene work, with several exercises as examples.

An Actor's Work: A Student's Diary, by K. S. Stanislavski (translated by Jean Benedetti; New York: Routledge, 2008). This is a modern translation of Stanislavski's *An Actor Prepares* and *Building a Character*, for those who would like a deeper dive into the "Method."

On Acting for Film

Acting in Film, by Michael Caine (New York: Applause Books, 1990). Perhaps the most well-known of all books on film acting. Mr. Caine is a master, and although he offers the perspective of a movie-star level that few in this business will achieve, it's a delightful read and full of good lessons.

On the Business of Acting

The Actor's Life: A Survival Guide, by Jenna Fischer (Dallas: Ben-Bella Books, Inc., 2017). Ms. Fischer's book is one of my favorites. For anyone choosing Los Angeles as the city to begin their career, it is a must read. She and I were in the same movie together (*Employee of the Month*), and although we've not met yet, I've followed her career and am a huge fan. Wonderful book!

Acting in Chicago: Making a Living Doing Commercials, Voice Overs, TV/Film and More (third edition), by Chris Argos (self-published by Tragos Ventures, Inc., 2018). A must read for anyone looking to begin their career in Chicago or the Midwest.

Being an Actor, by Simon Callow (New York: Grove Press, 1984). Mr. Callow's book has long been a favorite of mine. It is full of triumphs and reality checks on the life of an actor (e.g., unemployment: "the primeval slime from which all actors emerge and to which, inevitably, they return").

Websites

IMDb.com. This is a great way to search for information on films or television shows you are auditioning for—including actors, directors, writers, and producers. You can also manage your own profile on IMDb.com by signing up for IMDbPro.com (for a fee; pro.imdb.com).

ActorsAccess.com. This site works with Breakdown Services and allows you to set up an actor profile with headshots, résumé, and a reel. You can submit yourself on projects (for a fee) or have your agent or manager use your profile to submit you.

sagaftra.org. Website for the Screen Actors Guild – American Federation of Television and Radio Artists. This is a great resource whether you are in the union or not.

actorsequity.org. Website for Actors' Equity Association—the union for theater actors and stage managers.

~

Sample Résumé

Here's a sample résumé for an actor. It should be professionally done and sized 8" × 10" (the same size as your headshot):

Stef Tovar

Spire Artists Management/Stewart Talent
SAG-AFTRA / AEA
Height: 5'9"
Weight: 180 lbs

FILM AND TELEVISION (Partial List)

CHICAGO MED	Elliot Meyers	NBC/Dick Wolf Productions/S.J. Main Munoz dir.
WIDOWS	Finance Guy	Lawndale Productions/Steve McQueen dir.
CONTAGION	Dr. Arrington	Warner Bros/Steven Soderbergh dir.
PROVEN INNOCENT	Bob Callaway	CBS/Anna Mastro dir.
THE CHI	White Donor	Showtime/Jet Wilkinson dir.
EMPIRE	Doctor	FOX/Craig Brewer dir.
CHICAGO FIRE	Daniel Schwartz (recurring)	NBC/Dick Wolf Productions
THE GYMNAST (2006)	Dan	Flying Angels Productions/Ned Farr dir.
THE AERIALIST (2020)	Dan	Flying Angels Productions/Ned Farr dir.
EMPLOYEE OF THE MONTH	Kenny	Bull's Eye Productions/Mitch Rouse dir.

COMMERCIALS (Conflicts available upon request)

THEATRE (Partial List)

Off Broadway:

NO WAKE	Nolan	Route 66 at Greenhouse/dir. Veronica Brady
A TWIST OF WATER	Noah	Route 66 at 59E59 Theaters/dir. Erica Weiss

Chicago (select credits):

OSLO	Yossi Beilin	TimeLine Theatre/BIC/dir. Nick Bowling
THE ADVENTURES OF AUGIE MARCH	Clem/Nails/Oliver	Court Theatre/dir. Charles Newell
BOY	Doug	TimeLine Theatre Company/dir. Damon Kiely
MAMMA MIA!	Harry Bright	Drury Lane Theatre/dir. William Osetek
A FUNNY THING...NEW YORK CITY	Don	Route 66 at The Den/dir. Keira Fromm
APPROPRIATE	Franz	Victory Gardens Theatre/dir. Gary Griffin
BIG FISH	Edward Bloom	Theatre at the Center/dir. Bill Pulinsi
SOUTH PACIFIC **(Jeff Award Nomination)**	Luther Billis	Marriott Theatre/dir. David Bell
THE MUSIC MAN	Harold Hill	Paramount Theatre/dir. Rachel Rockwell
ENRON	Jeffrey Skilling	TimeLine Theatre/dir. Rachel Rockwell
NICE WORK IF YOU CAN GET IT	Cookie	Theater at the Center/Bill Pulinsi/Danny Herman
THE CHRISTMAS SCHOONER	Peter Stossel	Mercury Theater Chicago/dir. Walter Sterns
THE DOWNPOUR	Miller	Route 66 at Greenhouse Theater/dir. Erica Weiss
BOEING BOEING	Bernard	Drury Lane Theatre/dir. Dennis Zacek
MOONLIGHT AND MAGNOLIAS	David O. Selznick	Fox Valley Rep/dir. Dennis Zacek
RAGTIME **(Jeff Award-Best Ensemble)**	Houdini/others	Drury Lane Oakbrook/dir. Rachel Rockwell
ON AN AVERAGE DAY	Jack	Route 66/Victory Gardens/dir. Ron Klier
FIFTH OF JULY	Kenneth Tally, Jr.	Oak Park Festival Theatre/dir. Michael Weber
ASSASSINS **(Jeff Award-Best Musical)**	Czolgosz	Apple Tree Theatre/dir. Gary Griffin
BLADE TO THE HEAT*	Vinal	Apple Tree Theatre/dir. Gary Griffin
ALL MY SONS	Chris	Human Race Theatre Company/dir. Tony Dallas

Los Angeles (select credits):

THE LAST FIVE YEARS (L.A. premiere)	Jamie	El Portal Theatre/dir. Calvin Remsberg
SUNDAY IN THE PARK WITH GEORGE	George	West Coast Ensemble/dir. Calvin Remsberg
EVITA	Che	Theater League National Tour/dir. Sha Newman

Recipient: Jeff Award for Best Supporting Actor in a Play

TRAINING
Wright State University, Acting BFA
Voice Teachers: Roberta Duchak, Thomas Murray

SPECIAL SKILLS
On-camera acting coach; Makes a fantastic Kahlua Cake; Sam's Dad

Here's my résumé to use as a reference. I like putting a small version of my headshot on the résumé so that directors don't have to keep flipping it over during my audition to see my headshot.

Index

About the Author

Stef Tovar is a professional actor, teacher, and a native of Chicago, Illinois. His breakout on-screen role was Dr. Arrington in *Contagion*, directed by Steven Soderbergh (2011). Dr. Arrington treats Patient Zero (Gwyneth Paltrow) and must tell her husband (Matt Damon) of her death.

Stef's television credits include Elliot Meyers on *Chicago Med* for NBC (2020); Bob Callaway on *Proven Innocent* for CBS (2019); Daniel Schwartz on the premiere season of *Chicago Fire*, also for NBC (2012–2013); the 2018 season finale of *Empire* for FOX (giving some bad news to Jussie Smollett); *Boss* for Starz (2011); and *The Chi* for Showtime (2020) as "White Donor." Other film credits include "Finance Guy" in *Widows* (with Colin Farrell), directed by Steve McQueen (2018); Kenny in *Employee of the Month* (with Matt Dillon, Steve Zahn, and Christina Applegate), directed by Mitch Rouse (2004); Scott in the award-winning *Olympia*; "Studio

Exec" in *The Bobby Roberts Project* (with Fred Willard, 2018); and *The Gymnast*, directed by Ned Farr (2006)—as well as the sequel, *The Aerialist*, which premiered in 2020 on Amazon.

Select Chicago theater credits include Yossi Bellin in the Chicago premiere of *Oslo* with TimeLine Theatre Company at the Broadway Playhouse, directed by Nick Bowling; Clem/Nails/Kellerman in the world premiere of *The Adventures of Augie March* (adapted by David Auburn) and the Theban Shepard in *Oedipus Rex*—both directed by Charles Newell at Court Theatre; Harry Bright in *Mamma Mia!* at Drury Lane Theatre directed by William Osetek; Doug in the Chicago premiere of *Boy* for TimeLine Theatre, directed by Damon Kiely; Harold Hill in *The Music Man* directed by Rachel Rockwell for Paramount Theatre; and Edward Bloom in the Midwest premiere of *Big Fish*. Stef won Chicago's Jeff Award for Best Supporting Actor in 1997 for his portrayal of Vinal in *Blade to the Heat* at Apple Tree Theatre, directed by Gary Griffin, and was nominated for Best Supporting Actor in a Musical as Luther Billis in *South Pacific* at Marriott Theatre, directed by David H. Bell.

Stef was the founder and artistic director of Route 66 Theatre Company, which produced shows in Los Angeles, Chicago, and New York City. For Route 66, Stef was seen on stage as Jack in *On an Average Day*, by John Kolvenbach; in the musical *High Fidelity* (as record-store owner Rob); and as Don in *A Funny Thing Happened on the Way to the Gynecologic Oncology Unit at Sloan Kettering Memorial Cancer Center of New York City*. Stef created the role of Noah in *A Twist of Water*, by Caitlin Parrish, which opened in Chicago and ran Off-Broadway at 59E59 Theaters. *A Twist of Water* was made into a television show for CBS titled *The Red Line*, with Noah Wylie. Stef also played Nolan in *No Wake*, by William Donnelly, at 59E59 Theaters after runs in Chicago and Los Angeles.

Stef has taught his on-camera workshop at a variety of universities, acting studios, and casting offices across the country. He splits his time between Los Angeles and Chicago, and is the proud father of Sam. www.steftovar.com